PAKISTAN INSIGHTS
2019

PAKISTAN INSIGHTS
2019

Editor

Tilak Devasher

Vivekananda International Foundation
New Delhi

PENTAGON PRESS LLP

Pakistan Insights - 2019

Editor: Tilak Devasher

ISBN 978-81-941634-7-3

First Published in 2020

Copyright © Vivekananda International Foundation, New Delhi
(Pakistan Study Group)

All rights reserved. No part of this publication may be reproduced, stored in a retrieval system, or transmitted in any form or by any means, electronic, mechanical, photocopying, recording or otherwise, without the prior written permission of the Publisher.

Disclaimer: The views and opinions expressed in the book are the individual assertion of the Authors. The Publisher does not take any responsibility for the same in any manner whatsoever. The same shall solely be the responsibility of the Authors.

Published by
PENTAGON PRESS LLP
206, Peacock Lane, Shahpur Jat,
New Delhi-110049
Phones: 011-64706243, 26491568
Telefax: 011-26490600
email: rajan@pentagonpress.in
website: www.pentagonpress.in

Printed at Aegean Offset Printers, Greater Noida, U.P.

CONTENTS

Map of Pakistan	vii
Pakistan at a Glance	ix
List of Contributors	xiii
Editor's Note	xvii
Introduction by Dr. Arvind Gupta	xxi

INTERNAL

1	Pakistan Elections 2018: Military's Democratic Coup *Dr. Shalini Chawla*	3
2	Pakistan's Elections and 'Naya' Pakistan? *Amb. D. P. Srivastava*	12
3	Imran Khan: Political Inclinations *Prateek Joshi, Shruti Punia and Ankit Singh*	18
4	Pakistan: An Analysis of the Participation of Religious Parties in Elections, 2018 *Tilak Devasher, Shruti Punia*	22
5	Barelvi Assertion and the Tehrik-i-Labaik: A New Phenomenon? *T.C.A. Raghavan*	28
6	Pakistan: The Aasia Bibi Case and its Aftermath *Tilak Devasher*	33
7	Pakistan: Whither PML (N) after Nawaz Ouster? *Rana Banerji*	38
8	Pakistan-Significance of Pashtun Protests *Tilak Devasher*	48

9	The Pakistan Tahafuz Movement (PTM): One Year Later *Tilak Devasher*	53
10	Pakistan and FATF *Arvind Gupta*	72
11	Pakistani Economy: Challenges in 2018-19 *Prateek Joshi*	76
12	Emerging Situation in Pakistan in 2019 *Dr. Shalini Chawla*	85

EXTERNAL

13	Pakistan under Imran Khan: What's in it for Indo-Pak Relations *Lt. General S. A. Hasnain*	91
14	Efficacy of Track II Process in Indo-Pak Relations *C.D. Sahay*	95
15	Balakote and Its Aftermath: Analysing Pakistan's Strategic Elite Response *Brig. Rahul Bhonsle (Retd)*	104
16	Gilgit-Baltistan: Unclear Road to Political Reforms *Prateek Joshi*	117
17	J&K: Developments 2018-19 and Prospects *Lt. Gen. Syed Ata Hasnain*	125
18	Afghanistan: Different Possibilities for Ensuring Stability *Lt. Gen. Ravi Sawhney*	131
19	Afghanistan-Pakistan Relations: Frosty Neighbours? *Yatharth Kachiar*	136
20	Allah, Army and America in Pakistan's National Life *G. Parthasarthy*	149
21	Pakistan, Iran and Saudi Arabia *Amb. Dinkar P. Srivastava*	152
22	Conclusion: The Road Ahead *Tilak Devasher*	159
	Index	163

PAKISTAN AT A GLANCE

Area
Total (Land and Water): 881,889 sq. km.

Province-wise Area
Balochistan: 347,190 sq. km.

Punjab: 205,345 sq. km.

Sindh: 140,914 sq. Km.

Khyber Pakhtunkhwa (including erstwhile Federally Administered Tribal Areas): 101,741 sq. km.

International Borders
Afghanistan: 2,670 km.

China: 438 km. (via Pakistan Occupied Kashmir)

India: 3,190 km.

Iran: 959 km.

Length of Coastline
1,046 km.

Energy
Production of crude oil: 2,652,217 Barrels

Number of oil fields: 167 (July 2018)

Production of natural gas: 123,749 Cubic Feet

Number of gas fields: 181 (July 2018)

Electricity generation: 145,803 GWh (FY 2018), 119, 723 GWh (FY 2017)

(*Source:* CEIC data)

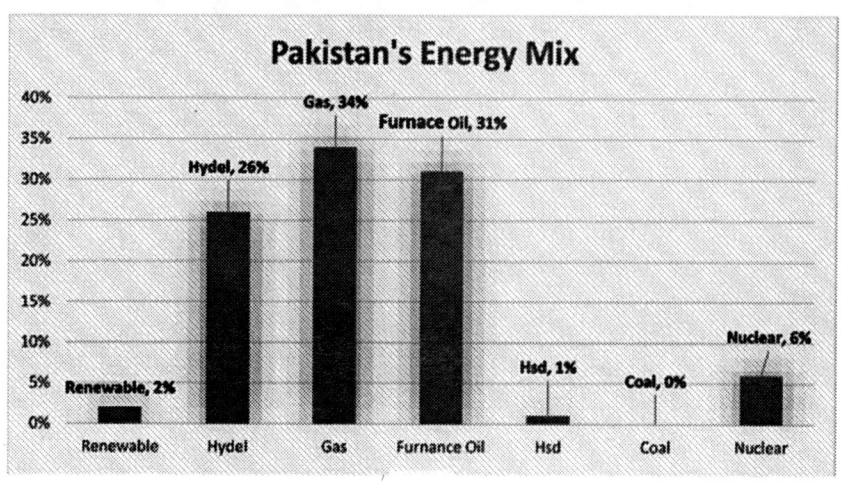

Source: https://en.dailypakistan.com.pk/featured/a-primer-on-pakistans-energy-mix/ (Hsd: High Speed Diesel)

DEMOGRAPHIC PROFILE

Population
207,862,518 (2017)

Growth Rate
2.4 percent

Population Density
242.9 per sq. km. (Britannica)

Human Development Index (HDI) (2017): **0.562 (UNDP)**

Province-wise percentage of population
Punjab: 53%
Sindh: 23%
Khyber Pakhtunkhwa (including FATA): 17%
Balochistan: 6%

(*Source:* Census 2017)

Religion

Muslims: 97% (Sunni, 77%, Shia, 20%)

Christians, Hindus and Others: 3%

ECONOMIC PROFILE

Economy General

Basic Economic Parameters

Criteria	Values
GDP (billion $) - 2017 [3]	304.95
GDP growth (annual %) [1]	3.29%
Inflation (March, 2019)	9.41%
Agriculture (% of GDP) [4]	18.9%
Industry (% of GDP) [4]	20.9%
Services (% of GDP) [4]	60.2%
Exports of goods and services (% of GDP) [1]	7.7%
Imports of goods and services (% of GDP) [1]	20.33%
Gross capital formation (% of GDP) [3]	16.094
Urban population growth (annual %) [3]	2.5
Energy use (kg of oil equivalent per capita) [3]	484.44
Electric power consumption (kWh per capita) [3]	471.04
Tax revenue (% of GDP) [4]	13.7
Personal remittances, received (million $)	19,689.00
Foreign direct investment (billion $) (2017-18)	2.767
Net official development assistance received (current US$) (millions) [3]	3005.15

[1] UN Data;   [2] PBS;   [3] World Bank Data   [4] Pakistan Economic Survey

INFRASTRUCTURE PROFILE (Pakistan Economic Survey 2016-17)

Infrastructure

Road Network: Approximately 257,000 km

National Highways: 12,131 km

Railways (Track Length)

11,811 km

MILITARY PROFILE (MILITARY BALANCE 2018, IISS)

Defence Budget (US $)

2016	2017	2018
9.19 bn	9.72 bn	1.11 tr

Force Levels

Active: 653,800 (Army: 560,000; Navy: 23,800; Air Force: 70,000; Paramilitary: 282,000)

Strategic Forces

Army Strategic Forces Command: 12,000-15,000

Air: 1-2 sqn of F-16 A/B or Mirage 5 may be assigned a nuclear-strike role.

Coast Guards

Strength: 4067 personnel (2016)

LIST OF CONTRIBUTORS

Dr. Arvind Gupta is a former diplomat who has served in Indian diplomatic missions in Moscow, London and Ankara. He has dealt with Afghanistan, Kashmir, the Soviet Union, Russia, and Central Asia in the Ministry of External Affairs. At present, he is the Director, Vivekananda International Foundation (VIF). He had earlier held positions of the Deputy National Security Adviser; Secretary, National Security Council Secretariat (NSCS); and Director General, Institute for Defence Studies and Analysis (IDSA). He is the author of *How India Manages Its National Security* published by Penguin Random House in 2018.

Dr. Shalini Chawla is a Distinguished Fellow at the Centre for Air Power Studies (CAPS), New Delhi. She joined CAPS in 2006 and has published widely in national and international journals on a wide range of issues relating to Pakistan and Afghanistan. She lectures regularly at leading establishments of the Indian Armed Forces and universities. She has authored three books titled *Pakistan's Military and Its Strategy* (2009), *Nuclear Pakistan* (2012) and ed. *India's Sentinel: Select Writings of Air Commodore Jasjit Singh* (2014).

Amb. D. P. Srivastava is a Distinguished Fellow at the Vivekananda International Foundation. A former diplomat, he was Indian Ambassador to Iran, the Czech Republic (2008-11) and India's High Commissioner to Malta. During his tenure in Iran, he led negotiations on Indian participation in Chabahar Port. After retirement, he served as Senior Advisor to ONGC Videsh Ltd for a year (2015-16). He holds a post-graduate degree in Political Science and Governance.

Prateek Joshi is a Researcher Associate with the Vivekananda International Foundation. He is working on Trans-Himalayan Geopolitics, Pakistani politics and Sino-Indian conflict. Before joining the VIF, he was working on a project with the Institute of Defence Studies and Analysis, New Delhi. Some of his writings have appeared in *CSIS, The National Interest, War on The Rocks* and *South China Morning Post.*

Shruti Punia was a young professional with the Vivekananda International Foundation. She has a keen interest in global politics, diplomacy and terrorism. She is a graduate in Journalism and Mass Communication.

Ankit Singh is an ex-intern with the Vivekananda International Foundation. He is a post-graduate from the University of Madras in Defence and Strategic Studies. He had earlier interned with India Strategic, Pravah. Currently he is preparing for higher studies in international relations.

Tilak Devasher is a consultant with the Vivekananda International Foundation. He is a former Special Secretary, Cabinet Secretariat, Government of India. During his professional career, Tilak specialised in security issues, especially pertaining to India's neighbourhood. He is the author of *'Pakistan: Courting the Abyss'* (December 2016); *'Pakistan: At the Helm'* (June 2018); and *'Pakistan: The Balochistan Conundrum'* (July 2019). All the books have been published by Harper Collins India. He is currently a member of the National Security Advisory Board (NSAB).

Amb. T.C.A. Raghavan is a former diplomat. He has served as the Indian High Commissioner to Singapore and Pakistan. He is currently Director General of the Indian Council of World Affairs. He is the author of *"The People Next Door: The Curious History of India's Relations with Pakistan."* (New Delhi, 2017).

Rana Banerji is a former officer of the Indian Administrative Services (IAS-1972, Assam-Meghalaya cadre). He retired as Special Secretary, Cabinet Secretariat, in October 2009. After retirement, Banerji headed a Task Force on Intelligence Reforms at the Institute for Defence Studies & Analyses (IDSA). He participates in the UN Human Rights Commission Privacy Rights Rapporteur's annual meetings on Accountability & Intelligence Reforms. He has participated in several Track-II and Track-1.5 interactions on Indo-Pak relations, Indo-US Security relations and Indo-Pak-Afghan Tripartite dialogue (2010-2015). His focus area of expertise pertains to Pakistan, Afghanistan and Islamic Terrorism.

Lt. General S. A. Hasnain, PVSM, UYSM, AVSM, SM, VSM and Bar (Retd) is a former Corps Commander of the Srinagar-based 15 Corps which is responsible for the security of Kashmir. He spent much of his service in J&K, both on the Line of Control, Siachen glacier and in counter terror operations. He is Chancellor, Central University of Kashmir.

C. D. Sahay is a Distinguished Fellow at the Vivekananda International Foundation. He is a Former Secretary (Research and Analysis Wing), Cabinet Secretariat. C. D. Sahay joined the Indian Police Service in 1967 and joined the Research and Analysis Wing, India's external Intelligence setup, in 1975. He rose to head the organisation from 2003 till superannuation in 2005. He has decades of experience in dealing with national security issues and international terrorism.

Brig. Rahul K. Bhonsle is an army veteran with over three decades of active service. He is an independent consultant on research and knowledge management in defence and security issues in the Indo Asia Pacific and Director, Security Risks Asia, a risk and knowledge management consultancy based in Delhi.

Lt. General R.K. Sawhney, PVSM, AVSM (Retd) is Centre Head and Senior Fellow, National Security and Strategic Studies & Internal Security Studies, Vivekananda International Foundation. He is a former deputy chief of the Army Staff and a former director of Military Intelligence. He is a post-graduate in Defence and Security Planning from the Royal College of Defence Studies, London. Post retirement, he was deputed by the Government of India to monitor the situation in Afghanistan, a country which he has visited almost every year since 2002.

Dr. Yatharth Kachiar is a research associate at the Vivekananda International Foundation. She is a Ph.D. from the Centre for West Asian Studies, Jawaharlal Nehru University, New Delhi, Her doctoral thesis was on "Soft power in Turkish foreign policy in West Asia and North Africa, 2002-2013." Her area of interest includes the Afghanistan-Pakistan region, West Asia, India and the neighbourhood.

Gopalaswami Parthasarathy was commissioned in the Indian Army in 1963. He later joined the Indian Foreign Service in 1968. He has served as the Indian High Commissioner to Cyprus, Australia and Pakistan and as Ambassador to Myanmar. He has also served in Indian embassies in Moscow, Dar-es-Salaam,

Washington and as Consul General in Karachi. He was spokesman of the Ministry of External Affairs and spokesman/Information Adviser, Prime Minister's Office (1986-1989). He was a member of the Naresh Chandra Committee for Review of National Security. Presently he is Chancellor, Central University, Jammu.

EDITOR'S NOTE

In February 2018, the Vivekananda International Foundation set up the Pakistan Study Group (PSG) to discuss and debate issues relating to Pakistan in a holistic manner. The intention was to go beyond the headlines to look at our western neighbour in some detail, at long-term issues plaguing the country and Pakistan's foreign relations. Meeting almost every fortnight since its inception, the discussions have been forthright and candid as also enriching and valuable.

Based on the ideas generated in these discussions, the Director decided to bring out a book consisting of articles written by members of the PSG.

Dr. Arvind Gupta kickstarts the discussions with an overview of developments in Pakistan in 2018-19. His broad thrust is that with the decline in the influence of the traditional parties and the rise of the Pakistan Tehreek-i-Insaf (PTI), the political landscape in Pakistan has been fundamentally changed by the 2018 elections.

The internal section has a host of articles that range from the elections in 2018 to the rise of the Barelvis and from the future of the Pakistan Muslim League-Nawaz (PML–N) to the economy. Dr. Shalini Chawla provides an analysis of the Pak elections in 2018 that she aptly calls 'Military's Democratic coup'. Two other articles, one by Amb. D. P. Srivastava on the elections and 'Naya' Pakistan and the other by Prateek Joshi, Shruti Punia and Ankit Singh on the political inclinations of Imran Khan deepen the understanding on the Pak elections. The blasphemy laws were in focus due to the Aasia Bibi case and the Editor tries to explain the case and its aftermath. While the focus has been on Imran Khan, Rana Banerji looks at the journey of former prime minister Nawaz Sharif and the future of the PMLN and especially whether he or any member of his family can make a comeback. There were two significant movements in Pakistan in 2018-19: the rise of the religious Right and the Pashtun protests. Amb. T.C.A. Raghavan focuses on the Barelvi Tehreek-i-Labaik while the Editor and Shruti Punia look the rise of the religious parties in the 2018 elections. The Editor looks at the Pashtun protests when they began in February 2018 and how they have developed a year later. On the economy, Dr. Arvind Gupta writes about the challenges that Pakistan faces from the Financial Action Task Force (FATF) while Prateek Joshi provides an in-depth analysis of the Pakistan economy and the challenges it faces as Imran Khan assumes charge. Dr. Shalini Chawla rounds up the internal section with an analysis of the emerging situation in Pakistan in 2019.

The external section looks at Pakistan's interactions with the key countries: Afghanistan, China, India, Iran, Saudi Arabia and the USA. Lt. Gen. Ata Hasnain writes about the prospects of Indo-Pak relations under Imran Khan while C. D. Sahay reminiscences about the Track-II process in Indo-Pak relations. Brig. Rahul Bhonsle explains Pakistan's response to the Indian attack at Balakote while Prateek Joshi explains the important developments that took place in Gilgit Baltistan. Rounding up the discussions on Indo-Pak relations, Lt. Gen. Ata Hasnain takes us through the developments and prospects of J&K in 2018-19. On relations with China, Prateek Joshi reviews the China Pakistan Economic Corridor (CPEC) at three years. Lt. Gen. Ravi Sawhney writes about the complexities of the Afghan peace process while Yatharth Kachiar discusses Pak-Afghan relations. Amb. G. Parthasarthy gives an overview of Pak-US relations while Amb. Dinkar Srivastava takes us through the complex triangle of Pak-Saudi-Iran relations.

In conclusion, the Editor tries to do some crystal ball gazing to predict the future trajectory of Pakistan.

The Editor would acknowledge the valuable help of Prateek Joshi and Yatharth Kachiar in putting this book together.

Members of the PSG are:

Dr. Arvind Gupta - Director VIF
Amb. Satish Chandra
Amb. G. Parthasarathy
C.D. Sahay
Lt. Gen. Ravi Sawhney
Lt. Gen. Ata Hasnain

Rana Banerji
Tilak Devasher - Convenor
Amb. D.P. Srivastava
Amb. T.C.A. Raghavan
Amb. Arun Kumar Singh
Rahul Bhonsle
Dr. Shalini Chawla
Sushant Sareen
Prateek Joshi
Yatharth Kachiar

New Delhi
June 2019

Tilak Devasher
Consultant - VIF
Member, National Security Advisory Board

INTRODUCTION

Arvind Gupta

After a struggle of nearly two decades, the Pakistan Tehreek-e-Insaaf Party (PTI) won 157 out of 352 seats in the Pakistan National Assembly and formed a coalition government at the centre. Imran Khan became the Prime Minister. The PTI formed a government on its own in Punjab and Khyber Pakhtunkhwa (KPK) and a coalition government in Balochistan. The Pakistan Peoples Party (PPP) formed the government in Sindh. Although it did not win a seat, the fundamentalist Tehreek-e-Labaiq Party (TLP), emerged as the fifth largest party by vote share. The rise of the TLP was an interesting feature of the election. Former Prime Minister Nawaz Sharif, the leader of the Pakistan Muslim League (N) (PML N), was debarred from participating in the election due to corruption charges and has been jailed. The PML (N) suffered comprehensively in the elections. With the decline in the influence of the traditional parties and the rise of the PTI, the political landscape in Pakistan has been fundamentally changed by the 2018 elections.

Army's Favourite

Analysts were of the unanimous opinion that Imran Khan won the elections with the help of the Pakistan army, which had no love lost for Nawaz Sharif. It was clear to everyone that Imran Khan was the favourite of the military. The popular jibe was that Imran Khan has been 'selected' as Prime Minister. Imran Khan boasts that his government and the Army are on the 'same page.' For him to continue in power, it is essential that he remains on the right side of his military masters. Imran Khan knows that, and he has taken care not to irritate the military. It is the military that now rules Pakistan through Imran Khan. This suits both sides.

Naya Pakistan

Fresh from an unexpected victory, a rejuvenated Imran Khan promised his countrymen to build a new Pakistan or 'Naya Pakistan". Attacking the misgovernance of his predecessors, he reminded the Pakistanis how the country had been looted by corrupt politicians and pushed into a debt trap. He highlighted the poor state of health and education in the country, drew attention to the epidemic of malnutrition among the children in the backdrop of crushing inequalities in the country. He promised a new beginning and a new Pakistan. He unveiled a highly ambitious populist agenda which included rooting out corruption, providing schools, colleges and hospitals, getting the economy out of the crisis, controlling wasteful expenditure, caring for the environment, building the stalled mega dams and so on. He promised a clean government and austerity on the part of government officials. He began his tenure by raising the hopes and expectations of the people of Pakistan.

Political Situation

No serious political crisis hit the country in the initial months of Imran Khan's prime ministership. One development that could have derailed the government was the crisis over the acquittal of Aasia Bibi by the Supreme Court on trumped-up blasphemy charges. Exoneration brought the radical hardliners of Tehreek-e-Labaiq on the streets creating serious law and order issues. Instead of handling the issue with firmness, the government gave in to the fundamentalist radicals by reaching an agreement with them. The government's concession to the fundamentalists may come to haunt it some day in the future.

Imran Khan has used the corruption issue to berate and undermine the opposition. Nawaz Sharif has been put behind bars. He has also stepped up his attacks against the PPP. The opposition parties, in turn, are blaming Imran Khan for ineptness as well as his links with the fundamentalists. They highlighted the worsening economic situation and mis-governance. The confrontation between the government and the opposition is likely to become worse in the near future.

Economic Crisis

Nine months into the government, the people of Pakistan are beginning to doubt whether Imran Khan's promises would ever materialise. Pakistan's economy is in a dire state. The treasury is empty. The growth rate is going down. Inflation is rising; the currency is depreciating, stock markets have crashed. Imran Kahn has been telling his people, "hausla rakhein", be patient.

He would be aware that patience can run out very quickly if the lot of the people is not improved.

The most visible of his attempts have been to go to China, Saudi Arabia, and the UAE begging for funds to bail out the economy. The government is also in talks with the IMF for a bailout package which will be the 12th in the country's history. But IMF bailouts come with tough conditionalities which mean hardship for the people. The Prime Minister cannot afford to reduce subsidies or increase prices of utilities and raise taxes in any substantive way for fear of increased disgruntlement amongst the masses. What Pakistan requires is hard-nosed reforms, but these would not suit the populist prime minister. His room for manoeuvre is limited. Pakistan's international image has been badly tarnished with the Financial Action Task Force (FATF) continuing to keep Pakistan on the grey list for its inability to curb terror financing and money laundering.

Foreign Policy

On the foreign policy front, Pakistan is struggling, but the Prime Minister has built a narrative of having conducted a highly successful foreign policy. Imran Khan has visited a few countries like China, Saudi Arabia, and the UAE and has, in turn, hosted the leaders of Saudi Arabia and Turkey. To Pakistan's disappointment, China has not given any relief to Pakistan by way of grants. Instead, it has rapped it on the knuckles for thinking about reviewing the China Pakistan Economic Corridor (CPEC) projects. There is a growing realisation in Pakistan that many of the CPEC projects are potential debt traps. Saudi Arabia and the UAE have given some temporary relief, having parked some money in the Pakistani accounts temporarily and deferring the payment of oil and natural gas. This has provided some elbow room to the Pakistanis. Recourse to the IMF seems inevitable.

Unexpectedly, Imran has got some relief from the pressure the USA has mounted on it because the latter is in a hurry to strike a deal with the Taliban and therefore needs Pakistan's help. The resultant softening of the US attitude is being seen by Pakistan as a big victory. However, the USA has not announced any financial assistance to Pakistan.

India-Pakistan Relations

Imran Khan has made Kashmir as the centrepiece of his relations with India. He has ignored India's concerns about cross-border terrorism. He was severely tested following the Pulwama suicide terrorist attack by the Jaish-e-Mohammad in which 40 soldiers of the Central Reserve Police Force of India were killed. Imran Khan handled the aftermath of the Pulwama attack clumsily. The world condemned in one voice the terrorist attacks conducted by terror groups sheltered in Pakistan. The international community's focus came on Pakistan which is sheltering numerous terror groups including Jaish e Mohammad and Lashkar-e-Tayyaba. The President of the UN Security Council issued a statement condemning the Jaish-e-Mohammad.

Imran Khan's lack of sensitivity to terrorism and its victims was seen by the whole world. Pakistan came under immense international pressure to return the Indian pilot who had to crash out when his MIG-21 plane was shot at but not before it downed an F-16 of the Pakistan Air Force (PAF). This was a major embarrassment for the Pakistanis who tried to enter India but were forced to turn back on account of the action by the Indian Air Force.

The international pressure for the de-escalation of tensions was seen by Pakistan as its victory. The reality is that Pakistan had no option but to de-escalate. Pakistan's economy was in no condition to endure a full-blooded war. Pakistan closed its air space for international flights. This short-sighted action would in the long run boomerang.

Pakistan was rattled by India's successful Anti-Satellite (ASAT) test on 27 March 2019. Its space programme is quite small, but its missile programme is fairly developed. The chances are that it would contemplate doing an ASAT test of its own some time in the future. It may seek help from China in this regard.

It is interesting that despite the Pulwama attack and other tensions between the two countries, Indian and Pakistani officials held talks to operationalise the Kartarpur Sahib corridor for Sikh pilgrims from India. India could not afford to suspend the talks with Pakistan because of domestic compulsions. However, Pakistan tried to include a few well-known Khalistani hardliners in the committee which would oversee the pilgrims travel through the corridor. This has irritated India which has refused to go along with Pakistan and postponed the talks further.

Pakistan's policy of supporting cross-border terrorism has not changed, as was evident in the Pulwama terror attack. Yet, Pakistan wants to show the world that it is acting against terrorism. It has launched a crackdown against terror groups and entities. Much of this is show and designed to satisfy the Financial Action Task Force (FATF). The experience shows that such crackdowns are ineffective and meant to divert the attention of the public as well as the international community.

Conclusion

Imran Khan's election has not brought any positive change in India-Pakistan relations. The deep state of Pakistan has got a pliable leader. Imran Khan is in no position to deliver on the promises that he has made to the people of Pakistan during his election campaign. The chances are that the economic crisis will worsen and the fundamentalist elements will become more and more important. He is not likely to show any let-up in the rhetoric over Kashmir. Nor is he likely to take any action against the perpetrators of terrorism against India. Pakistan will try to derive maximum benefit from the US weakness in Afghanistan which has compelled them to seek accommodation with the Taliban while bypassing the incumbent government. Anti-India rhetoric continues apace. The Pulwama terrorist attack and the Balakot airstrikes have dried up any chances of normalisation of India-Pakistan relations. Imran Khan has been consistent with the raising of the Kashmir issue at the drop of a hat. This shows that he is not serious about normalising relations with India. There has been no serious and credible action against Masood Azhar or the perpetrators of the Mumbai attacks. The Pak Army is simply not interested in the normalisation of India-Pakistan relations.

INTERNAL

1

Pakistan Elections 2018: Military's Democratic Coup

Dr. Shalini Chawla

Pakistan's General Elections in July 2018 brought in a democratically elected government consecutively for the third time, uninterrupted by a military coup. The elections very clearly once again demonstrated that the deep state in Pakistan has developed an implausible skill of controlling the nation without being directly on the political platform. The Human Rights Commission of Pakistan termed the elections—"dirtiest, most micromanaged and most intensively participated polls in the country's history."[1] On the other hand, Imran Khan's party, the Pakistan Tehreek-e-Insaf (PTI), unsurprisingly claimed that Pakistan witnessed the 'fairest elections' in 2018.[2] The elections did exhibit a struggling democracy and a clash of "democratic institutions" in Pakistan. *Freedom of Expression (Media)* and *Judiciary*, two important pillars of any democratic state came in direct conflict in Pakistan. There was obvious collusion of the military and the judiciary which supported the victory of the PTI and more importantly, defeat of the Pakistan Muslim League-Nawaz (PML-N). The elections were indeed distinct as compared to the previous two elections in 2008 and 2013, and did display noticeable trends which would have long-term implications on Pakistan.

Undoubtedly, the military continues to yield considerable power behind the democratic veil. A direct military coup does not benefit the military establishment anymore and controlling the state through a proxy government is far more convenient and credible in the eyes of the domestic and international community.

Civil-Military Relations have perpetually been a matter of great debate in Pakistan with the military dominating the core strategic decision-making process. During the 2018 elections, the military and Imran Khan complemented each other's 'vital requirements'. Imran Khan wanted to be in power and the military was pleased to support him as he appeared to be fully in sync with the military's objectives. The military's confrontation with Nawaz Sharif gave Imran ample opportunity to gather support within the military lobby. The 2018 elections were controversial and witnessed every possible dirty tactic by the military and ISI to ensure the PTI's victory. The elections were rightly termed as "Selection 2018" in the Pakistani media as the judiciary, the National Accountability Bureau and the military collaborated prudently to bring Imran to power.

Election Results: PTI's Victory

Nawaz Sharif came under the judicial spotlight following the release of the Panama Papers in 2016. Although Nawaz and his daughter enjoyed popular support, the Panama Papers put Nawaz Sharif and his family in probably the worst crisis he has experienced in his political career. Sharif, in his long political career, had fought many legal battles, but for the first time the allegations were based on reports by international journalists and not only the opposition.

Till the beginning of 2018, Imran Khan actually stood as a weak candidate with marginal popular support, as compared to the Sharifs. Accelerated judicial developments leading to Nawaz's disqualification and Maryam's conviction significantly improved Imran's position. Given the all-out support Imran Khan enjoyed from the military, the PTI's victory was not surprising in the outcome. The PTI emerged as the single largest party but short of a majority in the National Assembly. Although, the PTI's victory was anticipated, what was more interesting was the number of seats and the constituencies it managed to secure. The PTI managed to win 116 seats which were above the expected number, the PML-N emerged as a distant second with 64 seats and the Pakistan People's Party (PPP) won 43 seats. The Muttahida Majilis-i-Amal (MMA), an alliance of multiple religious parties, won 12 seats (Table 1). The PTI managed to form the government with the support of smaller parties including the Muttahida Qaumi Movement (MQM), Balochistan Awami Party (BAP) and Pakistan Muslim League Quad-e-Azam (PML-Q). Also, what was significant was the expansion of the vote bank of the PTI. Imran's party managed to secure 16.8 million votes as compared to 7.6 million votes it had won in the 2013 elections.

Table 1: Party Position in the National Assembly 2018

Party	Number of Seats
PTI	116
PML-N	64
PPP	43
IND	13
MMA	12
MQM-P	6
BAP	4
GDA	2
ANP	1
BNP	3

Source: Geo News, http://www.geo.tv/election/results. Accessed on April 13, 2019.

The party position in the provinces projected interesting trends. Punjab, the most powerful province, experienced a tough fight between the PML-N and the PTI. Despite Nawaz and Maryam being behind bars, the party managed to win 129 seats and the PTI managed to win 123. What was surprising was the PTI's victory in north, west and south Punjab. It managed to form a coalition with 179 seats with the smaller parties and independent candidates. Sindh was dominated by the PPP for the third consecutive term. Interestingly, the PTI managed to comfortably dominate Karachi and emerged as a major challenger to the Muttahida Qaumi Movement-Pakistan (MQM-P) in Karachi. Although the MQM did blame election rigging for their defeat, multiple factors including factions within the MQM-P and boycott of the elections by the MQM London played a critical role in the MQM's disappointing performance in urban Sindh. In Khyber Pakhtunkhwa (KPK) and the former Federally Administered Tribal Areas (FATA) the PTI was dominant. In Balochistan, the PTI had a marginal presence and the MMA and BAP performed well, which was expected. (Table 2).

Table 2: Party Position in the Provinces

	Punjab	Sindh	KPK	Balochistan
Total Seats	297	130	99	51
PTI	123	23	67	4
PML-N	129		5	2
PPP	7	76	5	–
IND	30	1	5	5

(Contd.)

	Punjab	Sindh	KPK	Balochistan
PML-Q	3	–	–	–
PML	3	–	–	–
PAR	2	–	–	–
BAP	1	–	–	15
BNP	–	–	–	6
BNP-A	–	–	–	3
MQM-P	–	14	–	–
GDA	–	11	–	–
MQM-H	–	2	–	–
TLP	–	2	–	–
MMA	–	1	10	9
ANP	–	–	6	3
QWP	–	–	1	–
HDP	–	–	–	2
JWP	–	–	–	1

Source: Geo News, http://www.geo.tv/election. Accessed on April 13, 2019.

PTI's Strategy: "Fresh and Clean"

The PTI's victory can be credited to mainly three factors. First, Imran Khan himself and his projection of a 'clean image'; second, the support he enjoyed from the military and third, the PTIs strategy of handing out tickets to electables.

The PTI began as a middle-class movement and positioned itself as a movement of the common man against corrupt elite politicians. It highlighted corruption as the main factor behind Pakistan's economic woes in its election campaign.[3] Imran certainly brought in a "fresh and clean" political face which did not carry the baggage of corruption, unlike, the other two mainstream parties—the PML-N and the PPP which have had a long history of corruption charges. The PTI's slogan of "Naya Pakistan" did manage to enlarge its support base and also attract first-time voters who claimed to be driven solely by the welfare of the state and wanted to give the nation a chance with a new leadership.

The PTI managed to gain 9.28 million more votes as compared to the 2013 elections. Electables played a major role and contributed close to 4.28 million votes to the PTI's vote bank in the 2018 elections.[4] Imran Khan managed to convince and give tickets to 46 electables, out of which 23 won.[5]

Although Imran Khan did garner support because of his promises of development, prosperity and anti-corruption drive, his performance in the first year has been disappointing. However, how far he manages to succeed in his promises remains to be seen.

Media Restrained and Suppressed

The intimidation of the media was probably one of the worst ploys in the election. Clearly, the military did not want a strong and assertive government that could legislate the judiciary and the military, according to Gul Bukhari, a social media activist who was kidnapped (for several hours) and returned blindfolded during the election period.[6] The military's position turned against certain sections of the media after journalist Matiuallah Jan published articles criticizing the military and judiciary.[7] Asad Kharal, broadcast journalist, was physically assaulted in public in Lahore.[8] Not only were quite a few prominent independent journalists threatened, attacked and kidnapped, the military tamed the leading media houses, particularly, the *DAWN* Group, *Geo News* and the *Jang Group*. The media houses were notified to drop articles by 'select columnists'. *DAWN* came under tremendous pressure after carrying former Prime Minister Nawaz Sharif's interview in which he confessed that the Pakistan military was behind the 2008 Mumbai terror attacks. The distribution of DAWN was severely impacted in many parts of Pakistan following the interview.[9]

Reportedly, the country's media regulator firmly cautioned the local news channels not to air any statements "by political leadership containing defamatory and derogatory content targeting various state institutions, specifically judiciary and armed forces."[10] Clearly, the ISI wanted to shape the media coverage to be able to impact public opinion and the vote bank.

Media mishandling during the election campaign did attract international attention and the International Press Institute, a Vienna-based advocacy group, described the acts against the media as "unprecedented" and "more elaborate than the attempts made in the past."[11] The attacks on the journalists were seen as "part of a larger plan to muzzle independent journalists."[12] Restrictions/Control on media is not new in Pakistan and the military leadership has always been against any form of freedom of expression that challenges its authority. The military has in the past cracked down on the media rather successfully to target its political rivals. What is commendable is that despite the threats and harassment, some sections of the media in Pakistan continues to fight hard to bring out an independent coverage of the core issue in Pakistan—*military's dictatorial role* and the persistent *civil-military struggle*.

Extremist Parties find Political Space

The elections provided political space to candidates representing jihadi and extremist groups despite ample controversy and apprehensions raised over the future implications of the development. The USA and the UN designated global terrorist, Hafiz Saeed's party, the Milli Muslim League (MML) was turned down by the Election Commission of Pakistan (ECP) after a prolonged debate. The Jamaat-ud-Dawa chief collaborated with a little known Allah-o-Akbar Tehreek (AAT) to contest the elections. What is surprising here is that despite pressures from the USA and the Financial Action Task Force (FATF) Pakistan did accommodate Saeed's political debut. The AAT Party did not manage to win a single seat, but this can be credited to the fact that it was created a few months before the elections and did not have time to expand its political presence.

The old religious parties like the MMA and Jamiat Ulema-i-Pakistan (National) did not perform well as compared to the 2013 elections, but new splinter groups established their presence.[13] The Tehreek-i-Labbaik Pakistan (TLP), a newly-formed party and an aggressive face of Barelvi politics, emerged as the fifth largest party which received 2,234,138 votes for the National Assembly[14] The Tehreek-i-Laibbaik Ya Rasool Allah (TLYRA) began as a protest movement and was registered as a political party by one of the founders, Khadim Hussain Rizvi, in the summer of 2017.[15] The group rose from the protests after Mumtaz Qadri's execution and came to limelight in 2017, when it blocked Islamabad for several weeks demanding stricter enforcement of blasphemy laws. Imran Khan supported the party and the TLP managed to get 2.23 million votes in the NA and more than 2.38 million provincial votes, which was termed as a "really spectacularly rapid rise."[16] The party targeted the PML-N during the election campaign and managed to swing a large share of the PML-N vote bank in Punjab. In Sindh, the TLP had an advantage due to division in the vote of the MQM-P. *The News* reported that political observers believe "that the MQM-London's call for boycotting the elections had affected the Urdu-speaking progressive vote bank in these constituencies, while the TLP mobilised its own voters to cast their ballots on polling day to have an edge over the MQM-P."[17] The TLP managed to gather the maximum number of votes in Lahore. The number of seats that the TLP won is not so significant, but what is relevant is a radical party's entry and performance on the political stage. This indicates the revival of Barelvi sectarian politics in Pakistan and is likely to have long-term implications for the state. Although lately the leadership has managed to control the TLP's aggressive positioning using punitive means, it will not be totally incorrect to say that Barelvi organisations will continue to try to increase pressure on the government through mass protests/other means. There will be an effort to employ sectarian discourse by these groups which will be a challenge for the state.[18]

What does it mean for India?

Elections brought Imran Khan to the helm and his stated vision for 'Naya Pakistan' was seen as a promising step. Needless to say, the PTI's promises do exceed its capability to tackle the challenges Pakistan is currently facing. The promises of development and economic uplift have come at a time when Pakistan is facing a severe economic crisis and mounting pressure from the USA. It would be interesting to understand how the 2018 elections and the PTI's victory is likely to influence India's relationship with Pakistan.

- Imran Khan came to power with the support of the deep state and (till now!) seems to be in sync with the military's strategic objectives. Imran's actions vis-à-vis India will be controlled by the military catering to the well-established strategic goals of the deep state. Hostility with New Delhi and the desire to stay at par with India has led to a drain of national resources depriving the nation of much needed developmental expenditure. Hostility between the two nations has continued and Islamabad's reluctance to give up sub-conventional war through terrorism has not allowed the bilateral talks or any peace initiative to sustain and succeed. It looks difficult that Imran Khan would initiate a change in the existing strategic dynamics and challenge the military's interests.
- The media was suppressed and not allowed to reach the masses during the elections. Once again, the military managed to control/direct the narrative domestically. This trend has been extremely damaging for the growth of Pakistan and also for India-Pakistan relations. Popular belief is driven in the direction to support the strategic interests of the military, which does not allow the core issues of national interest—economic and social development—to take priority within the state.
- Religious and extremist parties did find a political space in Pakistan

and got around 10 per cent of the total votes polled in the national elections. Although the number of votes is not significant, there is an expansion of the support base as compared to the previous elections. The trend is likely to continue and grow in the next 5 to 10 years, placing a larger number of religious and extremist party candidates in the parliament. This will further institutionalise the extremist parties and impact the socio-political apparatus of the state. Pakistan's relationship with India will have an additional extremist push domestically in the future.

- The trends do imply that Pakistan will continue to sustain its state policy against India. The military will continue to control strategic decision-making and shape the narratives domestically. Civilian voices in Pakistan supporting change in Pakistan's strategic choices and power dynamics are unlikely to make a visible impact soon.

NOTES

1. Ikram Juanidi, "HRCP pessimistic about free and fair elections", *Dawn*, Islamabad, July 17, 2018.
2. Amir Wasim, "July 25 elections will be fairest in country's history: PTI ", *Dawn*, Islamabad, July 15, 2018.
3. Zaigham Khan, "What is PTI's ideology", *The News*, Karachi, May 6, 2019.
4. Fakhar Durrani, "Electables played key roles in PTI's vote bank surge", *The News*, Karachi, July 29, 2018.
5. Ibid.
6. "Media faces threat abductions ahead of elections", *India Today*, Noida, July 26, 2018.
7. Ghulam Rasool Dehlvi, "Pakistan Elections: How Country's Judiciary and Military joined forces to gag media and influence public opinion", *Firstport*, Mumbai, December 1, 2018.
8. Imran Gabol, "Journalist Kharal beaten up by masked men in Lahore", *Dawn*, Islamabad, June 6, 2018.
9. Dehlvi, Ibid.
10. Drazen Jorgic and Mubasher Bukhari, "Ousted Pakistan PM arrested on return, as bomber kills scores," *Reuters*, London, July 12, 2018.
11. Katty Gannon, "Pakistan's media faces threats, abduction ahead of votes," *The Associated Press*, New York, June 26, 2018.
12. Ibid.
13. Ramsha Jahangir, "Religious parties clinch over 9pc share in National Assembly," *Dawn*, Islamabad, May 19, 2018.
14. Ibid.
15. Mossa Kaleem, "The emergence of Tehreek-e-Labbaik Pakistan on Karachi's political map," *Herald*, Islamabad, September 20, 2018.

16. "The rise and rise of Tehreek-e-Labbaik," *Pakistan Today*, Lahore, July 31, 2018.
17. Arshad Yousafzai, "Tehreek-e-Labbaik makes entry into Sindh Assembly with two wins in Karachi," *The News*, July 27, 2018.
18. Iqbal Singh Sevea, "The rise of Barelvi Political Activism in Pakistan," *ISAS Insights*, NUS, Singapore, No. 520, October 30, 2018.

2
Pakistan's Elections and 'Naya' Pakistan?[1]

Amb. D. P. Srivastava

The election for Pakistan's National Assembly saw Imran Khan's Pakistan Tehreek-e-Insaf (PTI) Party doubling its vote share from 16.32 per cent in the 2013 elections to 31.8 per cent. Its seat share went up from 28 to 115. In the case of the Pakistan Muslim League-Nawaz (PML-N), the voting percentage fell from 32.77 per cent in 2013 to 24.29 per cent, while its seat share came down more dramatically from 126 to 64. The Pakistan People's Party's (PPP) vote percentage declined marginally from 15.23 per cent to 13.05 per cent, but its seat share actually went up from 33 to 43. The results have evoked different reactions across the political spectrum. Though Nawaz Sharif's party has been decimated, Imran Khan has fallen short of a majority and will remain dependent upon the Army's support to cobble up and maintain his coalition in Islamabad. The results could not have been better from the perspective of 'extra-terrestrials', as Nawaz Sharif called the unseen hands guiding the pre-poll process.

Immediately after the elections, the Jamiat Ulema-i-Islam-Fazal (JUI-F) party of Maulana Fazlur Rehman called for a boycott of the assemblies. After mulling over it for two days and consulting the PPP, the PML-N conveyed that it would take part in the National Assembly session. The decision was, no doubt, driven by the calculation that the two mainstream parties hoped to save their hold over provincial governments in Sindh and Punjab. While the PPP has retained and consolidated its hold on Sindh, the PML-N's chances to form the government in Punjab, despite being the single largest party, seem tenuous. At the federal level, the opposition has announced that it will field candidates to contest the three key posts of Prime Minister (PML-N), Speaker (PPP) and Deputy Speaker.

Elections for the National Assembly were co-terminus with elections for the provincial assemblies. In Punjab, the PML-N emerged as the single largest political party with 127 seats, with the PTI coming second with 122 seats. To form the government, 149 seats were needed. Both parties are trying to attract the support of independents and other groups. Each has expressed confidence that it will get the majority and form the government. Whether Imran Khan has the maturity to give space to the PML-N to form the government in Punjab remains to be seen. So far, he has shown no sign of accommodation. In a similar situation in 2013, Nawaz Sharif had declined the offer of the JUI-F to form the government in Khyber Pakhtunkhwa (KP), upholding the democratic principle that the single largest party should be allowed to form the government. This helped Imran Khan's PTI to form the government in the province. The decision of the Pakistan Supreme Court Chief Justice to order a review of all major contracts awarded by the Shahbaz Sharif government in the last five years could be an indication that the establishment is unlikely to allow the PML-N to retain its hold on the country's most populous province.

In Sindh, the PPP has won 76 out of 130 seats, while the PTI has bagged 23 seats. The Muttahida Qaumi Movement-Pakistan (MQM-P) party has finished third with 11 seats in the provincial assembly. This is a far cry from the 37 seats the party got in the 2013 elections. With this configuration, the PPP does not need to take the MQM on board in the government. A drop in the MQM's seat share or percentage of votes polled is not simply due to a split in the party. Altaf had given a call to boycott the elections. The voter turnout in Karachi dropped from 40 per cent in 2013 to 29 per cent in 2018. This attests to his hold on the Mohajirs, whatever be the outcome in terms of the legislative process. The Karachi election produced a major surprise, where Bilawal Bhutto lost from Lyari, the traditional stronghold of the PPP. The seat was bagged by Abdul Saad of the PTI.

The PTI won 66 seats in the provincial assembly in KP with 32.5 per cent votes, Muttahida Majlis-e-Amal (MMA) party won 10 seats with 17 per cent votes and the Awami National Party (ANP) got six seats with 12 per cent votes. The PTI's victory was remarkable. It could overcome anti-incumbency and still increase its vote share. The ANP, once a major political force in the province, has been steadily losing out to religious parties. But such a dramatic change in the relative position of religious parties is difficult to explain.

The Balochistan Awami Party (BAP) emerged as the leading party in Balochistan, marginalising traditional parties like the Baloch National Party (BNP). The PML-N, which had formed the government in the province last time, lost badly. It is likely that the BAP, with some support from the PTI could form the government in the province. Whether they would bring into the legislative process the Baloch nationalist forces remains to be seen. The voter turnout went up from 42.8 per cent in 2013 to 45.27 per cent in 2018.

The impression that religious parties did not win enough seats ignores the fact that fundamentalism has been mainstreamed in Pakistan. The PPP and the PML-N tried to ward off the challenge of religious parties by adopting their agenda. The PTI went further. Imran Khan's statement after the election alluded to the ideal of Madinah for the Pakistan of the future. The change in the 2018 elections was in terms of votes gathered by new players. While the old, established grouping of religious parties—JUI (F), MMA—got 4.8 per cent votes, the Tehreek-e-Labbaik (TLP), a new entrant, came close with 4.2 per cent votes. This was the party that provided support to Imran Khan's street protest against Nawaz Sharif, and obviously had the Army's backing. Together, the vote share of old and new religious parties in the 2018 elections at nine per cent exceeded the combined vote share of the JUI-F, MMA and Jamaat-e-Islami (JI) at 5.8 per cent in the 2013 elections.

The TLP did not win any seat in the National Assembly despite scoring 2.231 million votes countrywide. Party candidates were fielded to divide the vote bank of the PML-N, which it has successfully done. What is more impressive, or alarming, is the fact that it bagged more votes in the PPP stronghold of Lyari than Bilawal Bhutto, the Chairman of the PPP who finished third in the NA-247 seat. The seat was won by PTI's Abdul Saad. Obviously, religion has a stronger appeal than social justice, which once used to be the PPP's message even amongst the poor. Though the party did not win any National Assembly seat, it won one of the two provincial assembly seats in Lyari. The PA-107 seat was won by Mohammad Soomro of the TLP.

Economy

According to an International Monetary Fund (IMF) estimate, Pakistan's fiscal deficit is expected to reach seven per cent against the target of 4.1 per cent. The foreign exchange reserve had dwindled down to USD 9 billion as on 20 July 2018 according to the State Bank of Pakistan. This is less than two months of imports. Pakistan is expected to approach the IMF for a USD 12 billion bailout package.² The US Secretary of State's remark that there is no rationale for the IMF and associated US tax dollars to go for the payment of Chinese loans drew a sharp response from Pakistani and Chinese officials. Pakistani officials denied that Pakistan has approached the IMF. The Chinese comment that the IMF has its own rules and procedures came with the advice that Pakistan should resolve the issues satisfactorily. This was an acknowledgement that a problem exists. In the meantime, the US Congress has reduced the Coalition Support Fund for Fiscal 2019 from USD 700 million to USD 150 million.

Asad Umar, who is expected to be appointed the Finance Minister in Imran Khan's Cabinet, stated that Pakistan's external debt is USD 95 billion.³ According to an IMF Report of March 2018, Pakistan's current account deficit has increased from one per cent of GDP in 2014-15 to 4.4 per cent in 2017-18. During this period, the share of Chinese debt in Pakistan's External Debt (non-IMF sources) went up from USD 551 million (out of USD 3,088 million) in 2014-15 to USD 2075 million (out of USD 6,144 million) in 2017-18. In percentage terms, China's share has gone up from 17.84 per cent to 33.77 per cent during this period. China as a creditor outranked the World Bank at 10.61 per cent (USD 652 million) and the Asian Development Bank (ADB) at 13.44 per cent (USD 824) in the Pakistani debt basket last year. The share of the IMF in external credit was low (seven per cent) in 2017 and declining thereafter. The IMF's influence over Pakistan's macro-economic policies would also be lower, unless Pakistan manages to secure fresh IMF credit. China could increase its leverage over Pakistan if it decides to go alone in the event of an IMF refusal. But then, it will not have the luxury of the IMF bailing out Chinese creditors.

The IMF report was part of a review based on the Pakistan Government's response and hence provides an authoritative overview of the health of Pakistan's economy. Since the report came out in March 2018, oil prices have shot up steeply following US withdrawal from the Iran Nuclear deal. Consequently, Pakistan's current account balance would have deteriorated further.

Geo-politics

Imran Khan, like his predecessors, will have to balance between China and the USA. He has identified Afghanistan as a priority. He has been invited by President Ghani to visit Kabul. He comes with baggage, which will make his role as a mediator in any dialogue with the Taliban suspicious to the Afghan government. Of all the Pakistani politicians, he has the most pro-Taliban role in Pakistani politics. He has a choice to jettison his domestic constituency, which has contributed to increasing his vote share in KP. This may not be a palatable option.

Imran Khan's post-election speech called for trade with India. This was in contrast to his fiery speeches on Kashmir on the election trail where he invoked the old UN Security Council resolutions. Shahbaz Sharif also made strong statements against India. We may grant that candidate Imran and Prime Minister Imran may articulate their positions differently. But the constituency he caters to limits his margin of manoeuvre. We could wait and watch how he addresses the Afghan issue. He will also need time, effort and luck to pull the Pakistan economy out of its downward spiral. Stabilising the economy needs control over defence expenditure and better relations with the neighbours. Successive Pakistani rulers came to realise this once they took over the reins of power. Yet, they have been unable to change the status quo.

Conclusion

The election results reflect the growing fragility of Pakistan's polity with the two largest parties—the PML (N) and the PPP—reduced to the status of provincial parties. The PTI has emerged as the only party with a presence in all the four provinces. But its victory may reflect an enduring role of the Pakistani Army and growing Islamisation of Pakistani society. Whether religion has ironed out the ethnic divide or that strand will re-surface only time can tell. Though the PTI has staked a claim at the Federal as well as Provincial level, it could muster a simple majority in only one province—KPK.

The Nawa-e-Waqt editorial of 5 August 2018 cites a Free and Fair Election Network (FAFEN) election observer report that in 169 National and Provincial Assembly constituencies the victory margin was much less than the number of rejected votes. A total of 1,670,000 votes were rejected during the counting. This included 906,000 votes rejected in Punjab, 608,000 in Sindh, 108,000 in Balochistan and 248,000 in KP. The report mentions that the rejected votes exceed the victory margin in 21 PTI constituencies, six PPP constituencies, 11 PML-N constituencies, three BAP constituencies and three GDA constituencies. Such cases include the NA-131 seat in Lahore won by Imran Khan. The editorial has argued that in all such constituencies, re-counting should be done.

The Punjab High Court has ordered a recount in the NA-131 seat in

Lahore won by Imran Khan by a slender majority. The court has asked the Election Commission of Pakistan to withhold notification of results of this seat. PML-N candidate Khwaja Saad Rafiq, who challenged the result, said that Imran Khan in his post-election statement has claimed that he was open to investigation in all cases. However, his defence lawyer has opposed re-polling in the constituency where Imran Khan's personal fortunes are involved.

'Naya Pakistan' of Imran's conception is increasingly looking like the old.

NOTES

1 First published by VIF on 8 August 2018, https://www.vifindia.org/article/2018/august/08/pakistan-s-elections-and-naya-pakistan
2 Kiran Stacey and Farhan Bokhari, "Pakistan set to seek up to $12bn IMF bailout," *Financial Times*, London, July 29, 2018.
3 Dr. Ashfaque Khan, "Drowned in debt", Business Recorder, *Business Recorder*, Karachi, May 17, 2018.

3

Imran Khan: Political Inclinations[1]

Prateek Joshi, Shruti Punia and Ankit Singh

The Pakistan Tehreek-e-Insaf (PTI) emerged as the largest party with 115 seats in the National Assembly, besides winning two-third seats in the Khyber Pakhtunkwa (KP) provincial assembly and emerging as the second largest party in the Punjab assembly with 123 seats, only six short of the Pakistan Muslim League-Nawaz's (PML-N) 129 seats. In urban Sindh, the party dealt a massive blow to the Muttahida Qaumi Movement-Pakistan (MQM-P) and clinched 12 of Karachi's 21 National Assembly seats, and is expected to form a coalition government in Balochistan. Both, Imran Khan and the PTI have come a long way, especially in these ten years, beginning with the PTI's boycott of the 2008 elections, followed by its relatively poor performance in the 2013 polls.

Almost 22 years after Imran Khan founded the PTI, the sea change is visible in the two eras when Imran lost on both National Assembly seats he contested during the 1997 elections and his present victory on all five seats he contested. For his admirers, the basis of Imran's victory lies in his natural leadership traits, strong will and his ability to identify talent that had also led the Pakistani cricket team to the World Cup victory under his captaincy in 1992, and the subsequent establishment of the cancer hospital he had pledged.

In the present context, the PTI has some achievements to its credit in KP, where its first tenure did result in improvements in the healthcare and education sectors, besides police reforms. Imran's popularity wave was strong enough to overshadow even the big ticket infrastructure projects that came up in Punjab under Shahbaz Sharif's tenure and the China Pakistan Economic Corridor projects across Pakistan credit for which Nawaz Sharif had been claiming.

An overall understanding of Imran's victory alludes to his gradual evolution from an emotional crusader to a pragmatic strategist who not only learnt to communicate with the masses but also transformed his support into victory by employing a set of means which he described as the "science of fighting elections." Nevertheless, his personal conduct has not gone unquestioned.

Unlike the PML-N or the Pakistan People's Party (PPP), which have relied on patronage-cum-ideologically driven mass support bases, the case is different for Imran as his supporters come from diverse backgrounds ranging from the youth to the aspirational urban middle class, the liberals as well as the conservatives. While Imran's Westernized upbringing and allegations on his personal conduct (including a tell-all book by his former wife) were overlooked to an extent that it did not dent the PTI's electoral performance, his support to the conservative parties has been very much open. He was credited with giving tickets to women in areas where no woman had even voted in decades. At the same time, his rendezvous with extremists and his view that "feminism degrades motherhood" helped retain his popularity among the conservative sections.[2]

In 2014, his sympathy for the Tehreek-e-Taliban Pakistan (TTP) made the group nominate him as one of its interlocutors with the Pakistani establishment although he backed out later.[3] Imran has been a staunch supporter of the Khatm-e-Nabuwwat issue too. Also, immediately after the election results were declared, the PTI was quick to reach out to Muavia Azam (son of slain Sipah-e-Sahaba chief Azam Tariq) to solicit support from the newly elected Member of the Punjab Assembly where the party vies for the required numbers to form the government.

Another trait of his that could provide fodder to the opposition parties is his tendency to take u-turns that have also made him a subject of controversies from time to time. His new found support to the Army, the decision to tactically back the PPP in the Senate elections and the decision to field "electables" despite their questionable backgrounds does not give any indication of him being different from the traditional parties which he accuses of being responsible for the present condition of Pakistan. Moreover, the PTI would need to tread cautiously as a strong opposition (which has questioned the fairness of the poll results) awaits it in the Parliament.

New Delhi too has its share of challenges. Over the years, as the PTI evolved into a mainstream party, Imran's views on India have become aligned with the structural constraints that define the Indo-Pak relationship. His erstwhile personal admiration for India has given way to a political cynicism that he has used to win the Army's support as well as target the Sharifs. Regarding his India policy, there had been apprehensions in the past over his hawkish views which were later confirmed as the PTI's election campaign repeatedly targeted Prime Minister Modi, followed by Imran's speech a day after the elections. Not only did he accuse India of portraying a negative image of him, but also indicated that peace and trade were conditional on resolution of the Kashmir issue. A few days before the elections, his meeting with Fazlur Rehman Khalil, an old figure in Kashmir's Jihadi networks, was another proof of how the new administration's Kashmir policy might unfold. Imran has also equated Indian control over Kashmir as a forceful occupation and likened it to America's invasion of Afghanistan.

Here, he seems to have repeated the Pakistan Army's line insinuating a possible surrender of the future government's external affairs decision-making to the Army. Given his views, it is still too early to write him off as someone pandering to the military's diktat, yet understanding his changing equations with the Army is indispensable, as it would form the basis of the future government's stability.

Some historical background is necessary if one is to analyse Imran's relationship with the Army. According to his former captain, Javed Miandad, Imran of the past seemed very apolitical who would shy away from political discussions and remained aloof. As his political views evolved, his disdain for the Army became visible when he would time and again accuse the Musharraf regime's post-9/11 foreign policy as well as the Army's role in propping up the civilian leadership. He termed the 2013 elections as unfair citing an understanding between the Army and the PML-N which ensured the latter's victory and named a former military Intelligence official, Brigadier Ranjha, as the person who supervised the job to ensure that the PML-N emerged as the single largest party.[4]

In another instance, while giving an interview to an Indian journalist, he went on record calling for establishing the supremacy of the civilian government over the military if he were to become the Prime Minister and added that he would prefer to resign if the military did not function under him.[5] He emphasised bringing the ISI under civilian control and an audit of the defence budget. During the 2013 election campaign, he even promised that he would order the Pakistan Army to shoot US drones if they crossed into Pakistani territory and insisted that the Army would be asked to withdraw from FATA where peace had returned and would bring in reforms to empower police and local government. However, the equation was to change once the Army's discomfort with the Nawazs became apparent.

In Najam Sethi's words, what appears as of now is a tactical adjustment between the PTI and the Army, whereby a large national party (accompanied by smaller regional parties and pressure group turned political parties) was needed to corner the PML-N.[6] The natural choice was none other than Imran whose hatred for Pakistan's traditional civilian leadership and specifically the PML-N knew no bounds, as was demonstrated by the PTI's four-month long sit-in in 2014 after the Nawaz regime refused to investigate the instances of poll rigging. The phase also prepared the ground for the military to choose an alternative to the PML-N in case the leadership became too big for its shoes, which it eventually did. As Imran is likely to officially take charge as the Prime Minister on 11 August, there is speculation whether he would complete a full term or face a similar fate as every prime minister in the past. His relationship with the Army would need to be closely observed.

NOTES

1   First published by VIF on 9 August 2018, https://www.vifindia.org/article/2018/august/09/imran-khan-political-inclinations
2   Shailaja Neelakantan, "Pakistan's Imran Khan says 'feminism degrades role of mother'," *The Times of India*, New Delhi, June 18, 2018.
3   "Imran will not represent Taliban, says PTI," *Dawn*, Islamabad, February 3, 2014.
4   Zulqernain Tahir, "Ex-MI official rejects Imran's claim of army help for PML-N," *Dawn*, Islamabad, May 5, 2018.
5   "Imran Khan says army, ISI will be kept under check," *Firstpost*, Mumbai, November 11, 2011.
6   Najam Sethi, "Welcome to "New" Pakistan!", *The Friday Times*, Lahore, July 26, 2018.

4

Pakistan: An Analysis of the Participation of Religious Parties in Elections, 2018[1]

Tilak Devasher, Shruti Punia

Elections 2018 in Pakistan would no doubt be remembered for the victory of Imran Khan. They were essentially a contest between the 'Naya Pakistan' and *'tabdeeli'* narrative of Imran Khan, and the *'vote ko izzat do'* and development narrative of the Sharifs. With the political engineering done by the Army, it was not surprising that Imran Khan's narrative came out on top.

However, the elections would be equally remembered for the appearance and significant performance of new hardline religious parties and its attendant consequences for Pakistan. This phenomenon marks a significant shift in religious politics and the use of religious sentiment in politics.

The 12 religious parties in the electoral fray collectively polled 5.2 million or 9.58 per cent of the total votes polled. Some analysts have pointed out that in the 2002 elections, the alliance of religious parties—the Muttahida Majlis-e-Amal (MMA)—had polled over 11 per cent. They had managed to lead a provincial government in Khyber Pakhtunkhwa, something that they were not able to repeat in 2018. Likewise, in terms of seats won, the performance of all the religious parties was poor: the MMA won 12 seats for the National Assembly (NA); 10 for the Khyber Pakhunkhwa (KPK), nine for the Balochistan and one for the Sindh assemblies; while the newly-minted Tehreek-i-Labbaik Pakistan (TLP) won two seats in Sindh.

It would, however, be simplistic to analyse the performance of the religious parties in terms of seats alone. For one thing, the elections saw the operationalisation of the 'mainstreaming' project of the army. This had been mooted in 2016 to give the *jihadi* and extremist groups legitimacy by bringing them within the political milieu amid growing international pressure against such groups operating in Pakistan. This 'mainstreaming' manifested itself in two ways. First, terrorist organisations like the Jamaat-ud-Dawa (JUD)/ Lashkar-e-Taiba (LeT) were allowed to set up a political party called the Milli Muslim League (MML). Even though it was not registered, its candidates were able to contest the elections on the platform of another party—the Allahu Akbar Tehreek (AAT). Second, terror suspects listed on the Fourth Schedule of the Anti-Terrorism Act (ATA) had either their names removed from the list just prior to the elections or were given free passage by the Election Commission of Pakistan (ECP) to contest the elections.

Second, the rise of these parties served a critical purpose in the elections. This was to divide the vote bank of mainstream parties. Even though barely a year old, the hardline religious parties fielded a surprisingly large number of candidates. The intention was not so much to win but to degrade the religious vote base of mainstream parties, especially of the Pakistan Muslim League-Nawaz (PML-N) as well as of the conventional religious parties to facilitate the victory of Imran Khan's Pakistan Tehreek-i-Insaf (PTI). This objective, as will be seen shortly, was well achieved.

Tehreek-e-Labbaik Pakistan

Tehreek-e-Labbaik (TLP), the political front of Tehreek-e-Labbaik Ya Rasool Allah (TLYRA), represents the Barelvi sect of Sunni Islam. Khadim Hussain Rizvi, called 'Hazrat Sahib' by his supporters, founded it in 2016. The purpose was to secure the release of Mumtaz Qadri, the security guard who had gunned down former Punjab Governor Salmaan Taseer in 2011. The TLP's initial appeal was based on its support for what Mumtaz Qadri had done. Khadim Rizvi was able to mobilise the religiously inclined lower-middle and working class with the slogan: *gustakh-e-rasul ki aik saza, sar tan sey juda* (there is only one punishment for the blasphemer, beheading). He got further support after Qadri was hanged. Finally, it was an amendment to the Election Act 2017 that altered the declaration forms of the candidates pertaining to the *khatm-i-nabuwat* (finality of the prophet-hood) that provided an opportunity to the TLP to expand its outreach. Rizvi led the Faizabad sit-in that captured the national imagination and enabled him to attract greater public support using the emotional card. The sit-in ended only after a senior army officer, Director General, Rangers Punjab, distributed money to the protesters.

A registered political party, the TLP, put up 566 candidates, including 178 for the National Assembly and the rest for provincial assemblies. It emerged as the top fifth party in terms of votes received getting 2.2 million votes for the National Assembly. It thus outstripped major parties like the Muttahida Qaumi Movement-Pakistan (MQM-P) and Awami National Party (ANP) among others. The TLP won two seats in the Sindh provincial assembly—one from Lyari's PS-107 and the other from PS-115 (Baldia Town). It also beat the MMA in Karachi. In Lahore, the TLP emerged as the third largest party in terms of votes after the PML-N and PTI on the 14 National Assembly seats of the city.

In the process of garnering 2.2 million votes, the TLP has almost decimated the other Barelvi parties like the Jamiat Ulema-e-Pakistan (JUP) that in the 1970s and 1980s were led by stalwarts like the late Maulana Shah Ahmad Noorani and the late Maulana Abdus Sattar Niazi. The TLP's performance for the Punjab assembly polls was especially remarkable. It fielded 262 candidates, including nine women, out of 297 constituencies. It outnumbered its rival religious parties by a big margin: the MMA got only 0.44 million votes in Punjab against the TLP's tally of around 1.9 million votes. In 88 constituencies of the provincial assembly, its candidates remained third and ranked fourth in another 82.

The party was clear that its electoral purpose was to thwart the victory of those who were responsible for the amendment on the *khatm-i-nabuwat* declaration. The target thus became the ruling PML-N since Barelvi voters had traditionally voted for them. Analysts have identified at least 14 National Assembly constituencies in Punjab where the PML-N lost and where the margin of victory was less than the votes polled by the TLP. In other words, if the TLP candidates were not in the fray, these votes would have gone to the PML-N and it would have won. Significantly, the TLP contested the election on its own and did not seek either seat adjustments or solicit becoming part of any coalition. As a stand-alone party, its performance gives a fair idea of its potential and strength.

The key to the success of the TLP has been two-fold: first, the Barelvi network of mosques and their prayer leaders and the fact that the majority of the population in Pakistan is Barelvi. Imams of mosques in various cities refer to Rizvi as 'Ameerul Mujahideen.' Hence, getting support in the name of a highly emotive issue like defending the finality of the Prophet-hood was not a problem.

Muttahida Majlis-e-Amal

The Muttahida Majlis-e-Amal (MMA) is the alliance of mainstream and long-established religious parties that is led by Maulana Fazl-ur-Rehman. The constituents are Jamiat Ulema-e-Islam-Fazl (JUI-F) headed by Maulana Fazlur Rehman, the Jamaat-e-Islami (JI) led by Siraj-ul-Haq, the Jamiat Ulema-e-Pakistan (JUP), the Markazi Jamiat Ahle Hadith and the Tehreek-e-Jafaria led by Allama Sajid Naqvi. The parties represented belong to the Deobandi, Ahl-e-Hadith and Barelvi sects of Sunni Islam and one Shia group. The alliance put up 595 candidates of which 191 were for the National Assembly and the rest for provincial assemblies. It won 12 seats with 2.2 million votes for the National Assembly.

The MMA was founded prior to the general election in 2002 that was held under Pervez Musharraf. The alliance, however, broke up in 2008 after the JI boycotted the elections while the Maulana formed an alliance with the PPP government. In the 2013 elections, an emergent PTI eroded the vote bank of the religious parties in Khyber Pakhtunkhwa (KPK). The fear of being further marginalised brought the religious parties together again in 2018. However, the alliance was badly mauled in KPK where both the Maulana and Sirajul Haq lost. In Punjab and in Karachi, the TLP and the PTI eroded their strength.

Quite possibly, the MMA constituents could have fared even worse had they contested from their own respective platforms. The defeat of the top leadership of the MMA is probably reflective of the disillusionment of voters with the mainstream Islamic parties. Likewise, the surprising performance of the hardline parties and the expansion of the TLP's vote base could be indicative of the voters being attracted to more extreme positions. At the time of writing, the MMA unity is under threat as a key component, the JI, is considering leaving the alliance.

Milli Muslim League

The Milli Muslim League (MML), the political front of the banned JuD/LeT, was founded in August 2017. Its allegiance is to the Ahl-e-Hadith sect of Sunni Islam. A total of 260 of its candidates contested the elections—73 for the National Assembly including Hafiz Saeed's son Talha Saeed and son-in-law Khalid Waleed and the rest for provincial assemblies. The fact that the photograph of LeT supremo Hafiz Saeed appeared on the campaign material used by the candidates made the connection between the LeT and the MML obvious. It was a thinly disguised attempt of the establishment to enable the JuD/LeT to be able to operate legally within Pakistan.

It is significant that Hafiz Saeed had earlier strongly opposed participation in elections, calling Western-style democracy as un-Islamic. His sanctioning participation in the 2018 elections is a fundamental break with the ideological moorings of the organisation that change in society can be brought about only through *jihad*. Clearly, the temptation of being 'mainstreamed' and acquiring political legitimacy far outweighed such ideological compulsions. Perhaps, the pressures on Pakistan of the Financial Action Task Force (FATF) and the necessity of showing action against terrorist groups like the JuD would have weighed heavily on the army that would have 'persuaded' Saeed accordingly. Though the party did not win any seat, it got 171,356 votes for the NA.

Assessment

The rise of the TLP in the 2018 elections is an important development that could have far-reaching significance in the future for several reasons.

First, the breadth and depth of the vote share garnered by the TLP and the other religious parties reflects a fairly strong reservoir of support for extremist thought in Pakistan. A comparison of its performance with that of the MMA would show that more radicalised elements within religious sects are gaining popularity. The fact that these hardline parties were part of an electoral process gives them legitimacy that will grow in future.

Second, the electoral empowerment of the TLP also elevates the Barelvis to the forefront of the national political scene. For long living under the shadow of the more aggressive Deobandi groups, they have now been able to mobilise their larger support base on an emotive issue that resonates with their supporters. Such Barelvi radicalism is likely to be more in evidence in the days to come.

Third, the entry of the Barelvi TLP and the Salafi MML implies that these two parties would now be contesting for the religious space in Pakistan that had hitherto been monopolised by the Deobandi groups. This contrasts with the efforts of the older religious parties like the Jamaat-e-Islami and the Jamiat Ulema-e-Islam as well as of their alliance, the MMA, that sought to bring together religious voters regardless of ideological differences. The implication of this development could be to further deepen the sectarian divide in Pakistan.

Fourth, Pakistan's first-past-the-post (FPTP) voting system, where constituency voting matters, has not benefitted the religious parties. Their support base is thinly spread across the country. It has been estimated that if Pakistan was following the proportional representation system, then the TLP could have got more than 10 seats in the National Assembly.

Fifth, given the kind of vote share that these parties managed in such a short time after their creation showcases that they will grow in strength from here on. In fact, some analysts were impressed by their election management skills in some constituencies. However, paucity of funds and trained volunteers were obvious handicaps. These could get rectified in the future.

Finally, 'mainstreaming' of terror groups per se is a laudable objective provided the groups are first disarmed, de-radicalised and re-educated. Without these essential steps any hopes of turning them away from terrorism and radicalism would backfire. In fact, the danger could be that having got legitimacy they would infect the mainstream religious parties too. These parties, for the sake of their own self-preservation, would have to match the radical rhetoric of the TLP. Likewise, the mainstream political parties may not be able to escape the pressure to move further to the right to firewall their own constituencies.

NOTES

1. First published by VIF on 7 September 2018, https://www.vifindia.org/article/2018/september/07/pakistan-an-analysis-of-the-participation-of-religious-parties-in-elections-2018

5

Barelvi Assertion and the Tehrik-i-Labaik: A New Phenomenon?

T.C.A. Raghavan

Amidst the numerous developments in Pakistan over the past decade and a half that have regularly punctuated its political chronology, there are those that also reflect structural changes underway in its policy and society. If a short list were to be made of these, the phenomena of 'Barelvi assertion' would certainly figure.

The Barelvis are so named because the movement originated in Bareilly in the mid 19th century. Their hallmark is popular Sufism, a cult of shrines and a deep veneration of the Prophet. They are therefore in contrast to the austere and literalist Wahabis and Deobandis. The founder of the sect, Ahmad Raza Khan (1865-1921), is a seminal figure of the late 19th century Sunni Islam in India. He had been an opponent of both the Deobandis and the Ahl-i-Hadith. That he stayed away from contemporary politics and was firmly opposed to *jihad* as armed struggle separates him also from the many other sects such as the Ahl-i-Hadith that mark Islam's response to colonial rule in South Asia. The Barelvis are generally regarded as pluralistic and adherents of a softer, more moderate approach although this image is gradually changing much like everything else in Pakistan.

For the past decade and a half there have been many signs of ferment among the Barelvis. The Canadian Pakistani preacher, Tahir ul Qadri, is of this persuasion and mobilised large numbers of his followers in 2014 to join Imran Khan's agitation. He thus demonstrated a street power in Lahore and Islamabad which rivals that of the Jamat-i-Islami. The assassination of the

Punjab Governor, Salman Taseer, in 2011 saw a cult following developing around his killer, Mumtaz Qadri, whose grave now is a Barelvi shrine in its own right. Two other related sets of activities—often very violent—exemplify this activism amongst many Barelvis: A zeal to act against real or imagined blasphemy and a fresh intensity to older prejudices against Ahmadis for disputing the finality of the Prophet.

What explains the larger churning among the Barelvis in this century? Since the 1980s they have felt excluded and disempowered despite being numerically preponderant in Pakistan, given the attention and funds the Deobandis and Wahabis have received since the Soviet *jihad* and as the militant and terrorist groups associated with them acquired a swagger under the benign care of their handlers in the Pakistani Intelligence agencies. Barelvi shrines were often the target also of these militants and perhaps this too contributed to the need to forge a broader and more powerful grouping. The role of the Pakistan military and Intelligence establishment is also pinpointed to explain this Barelvi resurgence. As their agencies battled the Tehrik-i-Taliban Pakistan and sectarian outfits in the first decade of this century there was a need to create new countervailing forces and the hitherto ignored Barelvis seemed the best bet.

Towards the end of General Musharraf's tenure as President of Pakistan illustrations of this process began to be evident. His calls for 'Enlightened Moderation', the establishment of a 'Council for Promotion of Sufism' and the appointment of Barelvi clerics with greater frequency than earlier to the Council of Islamic Ideology were all pointers to the thinking in the military mind of dealing with the blowback from extremist groups nurtured by an earlier generation of officers. Many linked Tahir-ul-Qadri's new prominence to this trend. These trends also received anecdotal confirmation from others. Most, if not all, mosques in Pakistan's military cantonments were of the Barelvi persuasion. Despite all the support Wahabi and Deobandi fronts received during the anti-Soviet *jihad* and later, it was ensured that these cantonment mosques remained insulated from their influence. That the Barelvis would appear an appropriate balancing force to rising extremism in Pakistan would have appeared a natural conclusion.

Yet it would also be a fair comment that while greater Barelvi assertion was visible in many ways in the first decade and a half of this century its political manifestation remained diffused till the rise of the Tehreek-e-Labbaik Pakistan (TLP) in 2017 coinciding also with a period of heightened civil military strife in Pakistan. The TLP came into prominence with and in response to a perceived watering down of self-certification by electoral candidates on the finality of the Prophet. Its 2017 agitation saw the resignation of the Pakistan Law Minister in the final act of a three-week long drama of a determined and religiously supercharged agitation in Rawalpindi and Islamabad. The Government, embattled and greatly weakened since Nawaz Sharif's removal, repeatedly apologized for what it said was a clerical error. Prodded by the Supreme Court, it made an attempt to clear the demonstration that had paralyzed the capital. This attempt failed and protests showed signs of spreading to other parts of Pakistan. Instructions to the Army that it step in to aid the civilian authority to restore order was responded to by a demurral from the Chief of Army Staff that efforts be made to resolve the situation peacefully. The resignation of the Law Minister was the final act of capitulation by the government.

The agitation ended with an agreement brokered by the Pakistan Army through an ISI officer. The details of the process gripped the public imagination as these events unfolded but in retrospect what had happened was a new prominence that the TLP acquired and, in the eyes of many, a new legitimacy. There was general agreement that at the vanguard of the TLP stood Khadim Hussain Rizvi, who exhibited during the protest and later, many signs of a grassroots, almost subaltern leader—his colloquial Punjabi regularly punctuated with humour and abuse certainly ensured the adulation of his followers. This fiery rhetoric was judiciously combined with a surprisingly good sense of the power of social media. Together with his followers, he articulated different strands that make up Barelvi assertion—a sense of victimhood, the frustration of the subaltern, and, most of all, the confidence that they form the most populous sect within Islam in Pakistan.

In the national and provincial elections in July 2018 this prominence of the TLP was visible as it emerged as the fourth largest party in Pakistan nationally in terms of vote share. It however did not win any seats to the national assembly. But the vote share is significant and in absolute terms it got more votes than any other religious party. Clearly the TLP has succeeded in aggregating under its umbrella a hitherto diffused Barelvi network of shrines, *pirs* and *sajda nashins*. But, by far, the most important outcome of the TLP performance in the 2018 election was that it played an important role in eroding support for Nawaz Sharif's party in Punjab and thereby securing his overall defeat.

In the post-election scene, the rise of the TLP appeared to represent three not directly related strands or processes—or at least so it appeared in analytical terms. First, a strong sense of Barelvi victimhood—that despite being by far the numerically preponderant Islamic sect in Pakistan, its social and political visibility at the national level was dwarfed by religious parties representing smaller minority opinions such as the JUI or the JI. This combined with the growing disenchantment within the Pakistan establishment with the direction of Deobandi and Wahabi groups, many of which were associated with radical extremists carrying out numerous terrorist attacks in Pakistan itself. The Barelvis could be a useful counterweight and counterfoil to this. Barelvi assertion could therefore be seen fuelled by both internal (to the Barelvis) factors and an external agency—the Pakistan establishment. Secondly, given the frictions that had emerged post-2015 in the civil military equation with Prime Minister's Nawaz Sharif's growing differences with the Army, the emergence of the Barelvis as a political force had the potential of leeching away grassroot support for the PML (N) in rural Punjab. For those who postulated that it was no less than a 'creeping coup' that had ousted Prime Minister Nawaz Sharif, the TLP phenomena was a confirmation of their hypothesis. Thirdly, Barelvi assertion, with the TLP at its vanguard, represented the larger process of mainstreaming of terrorist and extremist groups. In this view, mainstreaming of the Deobandi, Salafi and Wahabi groups made it essential that their future presence in Pakistan's political spectrum be balanced by other ideological strands of thought and in particular the Barelvis. This meant encouraging the TLP to aggregate to itself the otherwise diffuse political presence of the Barelvis in Punjab as also in parts of Sindh, including, in particular, Karachi.

These three analytical strands acquire credibility from numerous anecdotal accounts and evidence. This reached a peak with the manner in which the Islamabad agitation of 2017 was handled and in particular the drama of its conclusion. These anecdotal accounts acquired further evidential basis with the TLPs role and performance in the 2018 elections.

What has been the position since then and especially during the tenure of the current government led by PM Imran Khan?

In October 2018 the Supreme Court of Pakistan acquitted Aasiya Noreen of the charges of blasphemy for which she had been convicted and awarded the death penalty in 2010. This case, had in 2010 and since, attracted worldwide attention. The then Governor of Punjab, Salman Taseer and the minister for minority affairs Shahbaz Bhatti had spoken against blasphemy laws in the context of her case and consequently were assassinated. A massive cult had built up around the figure of Mumtaz Qadri, the assassin of Governor Salman Taseer. Among the many brave decisions PM Nawaz Sharif took, for which he possibly did not receive sufficient credit both in India and elsewhere, the decision to implement the death penalty on Mumtaz Qadri in early 2016 stands out. Mumtaz Qadri's cult following continued to grow after his death and very clearly is symptomatic of the larger and deeper Barelvi assertion in Pakistan.

In any event, and in brief, the Aasiya Noreen case from its very beginning has been closely related to the crystallisation of Barelvi assertion and resurgence. Her acquittal in October 2018 predictably sparked protests in which Khadim Rizvi and the TLP played a prominent part underscoring their new-found prominence. However, events thereafter have taken a different turn. Rizvi was taken into 'protective custody' in November 2018 and the TLP cadres have reportedly faced a 'crackdown'. Aasiya Bibi was finally acquitted by the Supreme Court when a review petition challenging an earlier acquittal was set aside.

Rizvi remains in custody and the TLP as a whole has generally been off the radar this year. This, of course, leads to the question of the structure of the Barelvi resurgence and its future. Can it be that its meteoric rise in parallel with the Aasiya Noreen case from 2010 has now come a full circle and will start ebbing with the final disposal of the case? Or is it that a combination of factors catalysed this assertion by Barelvi groups and they will now remain a significant feature in Pakistan's politics in the future? Can their political assertion in 2017-18 be explained by tactical factors and in particular civil military contestations and the need to erode the PML (N)'s traditional voter bases? Or is there a more structural explanation and that in turn derives from Pakistan's failed experiment with radical Islam?

Crystal gazing into the future of politics in Pakistan is hazardous. Perhaps a more useful way of addressing these questions is to widen the frame and bring into it some other hardy perennials of Pakistan's polity. The civil-military equation in Pakistan, the eventual outcome in Afghanistan in terms of the political architecture that will emerge there and finally the decisions the mainstream political parties, the PPP and the PML (N), take vis-à-vis each other—all these are factors that will have an influence on the future of Barelvis and how they position themselves in Pakistan's political spectrum.

6

Pakistan: The Aasia Bibi Case and its Aftermath[1]

Tilak Devasher

The controversy surrounding the blasphemy case of Pakistani citizen Aasia Noreen, better known as Aasia Bibi of village Ikkawali in Sheikhpura, Punjab, has drawn attention to the culture of extremism in Pakistan and showed the government and the army in a very poor light. It is only the Supreme Court that has come out with flying colours.

The Case

Aasia Bibi was alleged to have made three "defamatory and sarcastic" statements about the Prophet on 14 June 2009 during an argument with three Muslim women while the four of them were picking fruit in a field in Sheikhpura. The Muslim women objected to her touching the water container, saying that as a non-Muslim she was unfit to do so. Aasia Bibi was later beaten up at her home, during which her accusers alleged that she confessed to blasphemy. The women later went to a local cleric and accused her of blasphemy against the Prophet. Aasia was arrested after a police investigation.

A trial court convicted Aasia Bibi for blasphemy in November 2010 under Section 295-C of the Pakistan Penal Code (PPC) and gave her the mandatory death sentence. The Lahore High Court (LHC) upheld her conviction and confirmed her death sentence in October 2014. She challenged the LHC verdict in the Supreme Court, which stayed her execution in July 2015 and admitted her appeal for hearing. The hearing had been scheduled for October 2016, but was delayed as one of the judges, Justice Hameed-ur Rahman, recused himself from the bench. In October 2018, a three-judge bench headed by

Chief Justice Mian Saqib Nisar with Justice Asif Saeed Khosa and Justice Mazhar Alam Khan Miankhel as members, finally heard her last appeal against execution, eight years after being convicted. The apex court reserved its ruling on 08 October. On 31 October 2018, the Supreme Court acquitted Aasia Bibi, after accepting her 2015 appeal thereby reversing the judgements of the high court and that of the trial court.

Her case had attained prominence after the then governor of Punjab, Salman Taseer, met Aasia Bibi in prison in 2011 and advocated a retrial of her case. Subsequently, his own security guard, Mumtaz Qadri, gunned him down in broad daylight in Islamabad on 04 January 2011. Two months after Taseer was killed, Pakistan's religious minorities minister, Shahbaz Bhatti, a Christian, who spoke out against the blasphemy law, was shot dead in Islamabad on 02 March 2011. Qadri was executed in 2016 after the court found him guilty of murder.

The Tehreek-i Labbaik Pakistan (TLP)

On 13 October, five days after the Supreme Court reserved its judgement, the Barelvi Tehreek-e-Labbaik Pakistan (TLP) headed by Khadim Hussain Rizvi, threatened to paralyse the country within hours if the Supreme Court set Aasia Bibi free. The mother organisation of the TLP, Tehreek-i Labbaik Ya Rasool Allah (TLYR) had been set up in the wake of the hanging of Mumtaz Qadri in 2016. The TLP was registered as a political party and it shot into prominence after its strong showing in a by-election in Lahore in 2017. Later, it paralysed the federal capital in November 2017, protesting against supposed changes in the oath of legislators. In the July 2018 general elections, though the TLP did not win any National Assembly seats, it garnered over 22 lakh votes and became the fifth largest political party in Pakistan.

Rejecting the Supreme Court verdict that acquitted Aasia Bibi, the TLP began protests in Lahore on 31 October blocking main arteries and paralysing the traffic. Soon the protests spread to other important cities like Islamabad, Rawalpindi, Gujrat, Gujranwala, Lahore, Kasur, Okara, Faisalabad, Multan, Hyderabad, Karachi, Peshawar, etc. Other religious parties like the Jamait-ul Ulema Islam-Fazl (JUI-F), Jamaat-i Islami (JI), Jamaat-ud Dawa (JuD) of Hafiz Saeed, Jamaat-ulema Pakistan (JUP), and Markazi Jamiat Ahle Hadith (MJAH) also rejected the three-judge order and decided to join the protest from Friday, 02 November.

In a nation-wide address on 31 October, Imran Khan warned that the

Government would fulfil its responsibility to ensure its writ. He criticised the language used by a "small segment" in reaction to the verdict adding that the language used against the Supreme Court judges, the army chief and other important personalities was intolerable. Similar bravado was displayed by the Information Minister who warned the protesters not to ever consider the state to be weak.

However, the bravado lasted less than 24 hours. Imran Khan left the country a day before his originally scheduled date. The violent protests that ensued forced the Government to make a submissive agreement with protestors, agreeing not to oppose a review petition filed against the Supreme Court judgement, set free the arrested protestors, and, above all, set in motion a legal process to put Aasia Bibi's name on the country's Exit Control List (ECL) to prevent her from leaving the country. All that the government got in return was the TLP agreeing to call off the protests and a farcical apology if it 'hurt the sentiments or inconvenienced anyone without reason'.[2] No remorse was expressed about its calling for the killing of the judges or asking the army to mutiny against the army chief.

In a nutshell, instead of enforcing the law, the Imran Khan government was seen to have not merely capitulated but set yet another dangerous precedent for the future. The Government's claim that the agreement restored peace had few takers against the backdrop of the appeasement that was seen as having seriously dented the authority of the state. The zealots have been furthered strengthened and emboldened. The message to them was that they could continue to spew venom and indulge in violence and the state would meekly cave in.

What constrains the ruling Pakistan Tehrik-i-Insaf (PTI) from dealing with religious protests firmly is its own past history. The PTI was the one political party that had justified the TLP's Islamabad siege in 2017 and supported its demand that the law minister resign. Ministers like the Punjab Information Minister have even visited the grave of Mumtaz Qadri and paid homage to the executed murderer. Several leaders have attended rallies of extremist sectarian groups and not shied away from playing the religious card in the elections.

The Army too has been seen as weak when faced with the venom hurled against it by the TLP. In the face of an open incitement to mutiny, all that the normally voluble spokesman could say was that the military would not intervene.

Blasphemy Law

The blasphemy law in Pakistan dates back to 1860 when it was made a crime to disturb a religious assembly, trespass on burial grounds, insult religious beliefs or intentionally destroy or defile a place or an object of worship, punishable by up to 10 years in jail. In the 1980s, Zia-ul Haq added sections 295-B and 295-C to the PPC that prescribed life imprisonment for 'wilful' desecration of the Quran, 'death, or imprisonment for life' for blasphemy against the Prophet. This allowed religious extremists to spread hatred, incite and provoke violence and even kill people in the name of religion.

Statistics collected by the Lahore-based Centre for Social Justice show that a disproportionate number of minorities, relative to their population, have been accused of blasphemy. Of the 1,472 people charged under the blasphemy laws between 1987 and 2016, nearly 730 were Muslims, 501 were Ahmadis, 205 were Christians and 26 were Hindus. So far, no one has been actually executed for blasphemy. Most have had their sentences overturned or commuted on appeal. In the majority of the cases, the higher courts have determined that the complaint, the investigation and the evidence were fabricated based on personal or political vendettas. According to recent studies by Amnesty International, 'the blasphemy law is widely abused to perpetrate hate crimes based on religion, regulate personal vendettas and perpetrate economic injustice'.[3]

The Future

The ordeal is not over. At the time of writing, the complainant in the case, Qazi Muhammad Salam, has filed a review petition in the Supreme Court against Aasia Bibi's acquittal. He had also demanded that her name be put on the Exit Control List. While she has been freed from jail, there are conflicting reports whether she is still in the country or has proceeded abroad. Despite her acquittal, as *The Guardian* put it, "She may have been freed, but she's never likely to be free.... She will spend the rest of her days looking over her shoulder in fear of an international assassin."[4]

The outcome of the review petition will have a bearing not only on the future of Aasia Bibi but would be another test for the judiciary and the government. Having witnessed the impact of their decision, pressure on the same judges dealing with the review would be enormous. The three judges and especially Justice Khosa, who had heard blasphemy-related cases in the past and had confirmed Mumtaz Qadri's death penalty, would be at risk from *the* fanatics looking for revenge. Soon after the judgement, a TLP leader, Afzal Qadri had declared the judges *'wajabul katl'* (worthy of killing) and called upon their domestics to kill them.

The moot question is whether the government that has caved in once and is known for its 'U' turns is capable and willing to uphold the rule of law? And will the army that looms larger than life in Pakistan continue to ignore slurs on its chief and calls to mutiny?

Analysis

Pakistan will confront the legacy of the case for a long time. The verdict and its continuing aftermath will play a critical role in shaping the future narrative on blasphemy cases and extremist religious groups. In fact, this case has already become a test case for Pakistan, both legally and for the society at large. Legally, it represents the uncomfortable fact that the lower judiciary and even the High Court are unable to resist pressures from hard-line groups even though the evidence is flimsy, tainted and doctored. Incremental and increasing Islamisation in Pakistan has led to a situation where even a flimsy allegation of blasphemy can result in mayhem and widespread destruction of property. Socially, it represents the depth of intolerance and extremism that has developed in Pakistan and the kind of insecurity that the minorities face on a daily basis.

Clearly, the space for Pakistan to be a tolerant country is rapidly shrinking.[5]

NOTES

1. First published by VIF on 13 November 2018, https://www.vifindia.org/article/2018/november/13/pakistan-the-aasia-bibi-case-and-its-aftermath
2. Rana Bilal, "Government, TLP reach agreement; state to take legal measures to place Asia Bibi's name on ECL", *Dawn*, Islamabad, November 2, 2018.
3. Wasim Abbasi, "No execution under blasphemy law in Pakistan so far", *The News*, Karachi, November 1, 2018.
4. Harriet Sherwood, "Quashing of Aasia Bibi's blasphemy charge will not end her suffering", *The Guardian*, October 31, 2018.
5. For a detailed discussion on the subject see *Pakistan: Courting the Abyss*, Harper Collins Publishers, Noida, 2016, pp. 143-164.

7

Pakistan: Whither PML (N) after Nawaz Ouster?

Rana Banerji

Pakistan's stuttering experiments with democracy over the last 70 years have always fallen flat at the altar of military dictators. The military's domination of civilian politicians has more often than not been direct and brutal, at best in more benign times, tolerant of reluctant power-sharing agreements with civilian governments. Political analysts have categorized this as 'praetorian democracy'.[1] Every time military dictators took over power subverting the nascent democratic process, they promised to restore democracy after the proverbial 'ninety days'. This deadline kept getting deferred. A 'King's Party' would be floated every time to herald in a 'controlled transition' to civilian governance.

Nawaz Sharif himself emerged in politics as 'a blue-eyed scion' of Gen Zia-ul-Haq in 1985, when the latter felt the need to respond to the Movement for Restoration of Democracy (MRD) agitation of the early 1980s by appointing a Majlis-e-Shura. Nawaz's father, Mian Mohd Sharif, ran the Ittefaq Foundry in Lahore which Bhutto had nationalised. Zia undid the nationalisation and returned the foundry to the Sharif family.

Before entering politics in the 1970s, Nawaz Sharif studied business at Government College and Law at the University of Punjab. In 1981, he was appointed by President Zia as the Minister of Finance for the province of Punjab. Backed by a loose coalition of conservatives, Sharif was elected as the Chief Minister of Punjab in 1985.

When Benazir came to power in the 1988 elections after Zia's death in a plane crash, Sharif led the conservative Islamic Democratic Alliance (IDA). He was helped by the Army to become the 12th prime minister of Pakistan in 1990. Serving army officers and ISI agents engaged in conspiring against Benazir's election campaign and channelised money to the Islamic Democratic Alliance (IDA) in what came to be known as the Mehrangate scandal.[2]

At this time, the Pakistan Muslim League (PML—later PML-Nawaz) was very much the favoured 'King's Party'.

Nawaz-Confrontation with Military and Repeated 'Comebacks'

Subsequently though, Nawaz Sharif bucked the trend of falling prey to the mercy of military dictators for the next three decades and became the quintessential 'comeback kid' of Pakistani politics.

During Sharif's first premiership from November 1990 to July 1993, when Gen Asif Nawaz was the Army Chief, several issues of discord came up. Asif Nawaz had to sometimes cater to unwarranted recommendations on postings and promotions of senior officers. Apprised about rumours circulating that the Ittefaq group was distributing BMW cars as 'Abba ji's (Nawaz Sharif's father, Mian Mohd Sharif) gifts' to cultivate gullible Generals, the Army Chief confronted Nawaz, who did not deny the allegation, rather he offered the keys of a new BMW to Asif Nawaz urging him not to keep driving his old Toyota Corona as it was not 'befitting' for the Chief! Asif Nawaz politely returned the keys and walked away.[3]

When Asif Nawaz died suddenly after a heart attack in January 1993, there were allegations of arsenic poisoning. His wife later alleged that waiters at Nawaz Sharif's Raiwind house had claimed use of special 'poisoned' cloth to polish plates on which the Army Chief was served refreshments. Though Asif Nawaz's body was exhumed and an inquiry held by US forensic experts, these allegations could not be substantiated.

When Gen Abdul Waheed Kakar was appointed the next Army Chief, Nawaz Sharif did not agree with President Ghulam Ishaq Khan's choice. Relations between the two soured further, leading to Nawaz's dismissal in April 1993 under Art. 58(2) (b) of the Constitution. Nawaz challenged this in court and Supreme Court Chief Justice Nasim Hassan Shah deemed the dismissal illegal.[4] Later, the Army Chief, Gen Kakar, had to mediate, leading to a situation where both Ghulam Ishaq Khan and Nawaz Sharif were made to resign and Pakistan went into fresh elections which brought Benazir Bhutto back for her second tenure as PM.[5]

In the 1997 National Assembly elections, Nawaz Sharif's PML (N) received a massive mandate—45.9 per cent votes and 155/207 seats, with the PPP getting only 18 seats. This brought to the fore Nawaz's authoritarian streak—he introduced the 13th Amendment doing away with the President's powers to dismiss the PM and dissolve Assemblies.

A new chapter of confrontation was opened by the Supreme Court Chief Justice, Sajjad Ali Shah, whose court was stormed by PML (N) supporters. The Army Chief, Gen Karamat, refrained from responding to Justice Shah's call for assistance from the Army.[6] More differences surfaced. Lt. Gen Khwaja Ziauddin Butt was brought in as the new DG, ISI, once again without approval of the Army Chief. In a speech at the Naval Staff College, Lahore, in October 1998, Karamat criticized the profligacy of certain grandiose civilian government schemes and demanded setting up of a National Security Council. This incensed Nawaz Sharif and he called in the Chief to remonstrate. Karamat quit as Chief.[7]

Nawaz appointed Musharraf as the new COAS, over the heads of two seniors—Chief of General Staff Ali Kuli Khan Khattak and Lt Gen Khalid Nawaz Malik—ostensibly because he was a Mohajir. Nawaz believed, mistakenly as it turned out, that being a Mohajir, Musharraf would not be too dominating and Nawaz could reach over his head to appeal to Punjabi Other Ranks and officers.

Ousted in October, 1999 by Musharraf's military takeover, Nawaz was made to go to Attock jail in chains.[8] He served in prison briefly before the Saudi monarch interceded on his behalf. After remaining in exile for almost a decade, Nawaz returned to politics in 2011 and led his party to victory for a third time in 2013.

The 2013 elections marked a significant political watershed in Pakistan representing the first ever smooth transition to a newly-elected civilian government without military intervention. The Pakistan Muslim League (PML-N) won 129 seats out of 272 elected seats in the National Assembly, with 118 from Punjab alone.

Though Nawaz Sharif appeared to have learnt some lessons well about not ruffling the feathers of the Army unduly, he kept chafing at the bit during his third tenure, not having full control of power, especially in the realm of security and foreign policies.

Matters came to head with the *Dawn* leaks case in October, 2016. The *Dawn* newspaper alleged *that Foreign Secretary Aijaz Chaudhry told a 'closed door' meeting in PMO that Pakistan was facing diplomatic isolation internationally because it was not changing its policy of abetting 'non-state' actors selectively to sponsor terror in neighbouring countries. China had reiterated support to stonewall Masood Azhar's banning as a terrorist in UN forums but advised Pakistan to change its policy. Punjab CM Shahbaz Sharif and DG, ISI Lt. Gen Rizwan Akhtar were present in this meeting, apart from the PM himself. When DG, ISI suggested there was no difficulty in arresting any groups involved, Shahbaz Sharif claimed the Army was not allowing a free hand to the Punjab police. The report created a furore. Despite denials from PMO and the Punjab CM's office, the Military leadership was furious and commented adversely at their Corps Commanders' meeting about a major security breach.* On October 14, an ISPR press release, citing comments at this meeting, stated that the "feeding of a false and fabricated story of an important security meeting at the PM House was a breach of national security."

Dawn's reporter, Cyril Almeida, who carried this story, was temporarily put on an Exit Control List before the Press Corps protested.

Ultimately, the PM had to assuage the offended Army Generals by setting up an Enquiry Committee, headed by a retired High Court Judge, Amir Raza Khan and including officers from ISI and MI. In April 2017, Information Minister, Pervaiz Rashid, a close loyalist of the Sharif family was forced to resign (April 29), owning responsibility for the 'lapse'. Two other senior officials were held culpable. The PMO issued a notification dismissing Rao Tehsin Ali, Principal Information Officer in the PMO and Tareq Fatemi, Special Assistant to PM. Respected PPP politician and lawyer, Aitzaz Ahsan claimed they were made scapegoats whereas the real person/body behind the media leak was Maryam Nawaz's 'Media Cell' in the PML (N), whom the civilian leadership was trying hard to protect.

However, the DG, ISPR Maj Gen Asif Ghafoor issued a tweet rejecting the PMO Notification. A single tweet (later withdrawn) had yet again exposed the existing fault lines in Pakistan's power structure. The Army's refusal to accept the Dawn leaks decision showed how an institution with a coup-making past simply will not accept civilian supremacy, especially on matters pertaining to national security and foreign policy.

The 'Panama Papers' case[9] emerged at this time wherein it was seen that Mr. Sharif's three children—Hassan, Hussain and Maryam—headed companies that owned four luxury flats in London's Park Lane neighborhood. Daughter Maryam, now being seen as his likely political successor, was listed as the owner of two British Virgin Islands-based shell companies—Nielsen Enterprises Limited and Nescoll Limited—which were set up in the early 1990s, just after her father's first term as prime minister ended. She was underage at the time. Maryam and Hasan Nawaz Sharif signed the paperwork in 2007 that was part of a series of transactions in which Deutsche Bank Geneva lent up to $13.8 million to the companies with their London properties as collateral. Hasan Nawaz Sharif was listed as the director of another British Virgin Islands registered company, Hangon Property Holdings Limited.

Nawaz Sharif was not directly involved in the business interactions detailed in the documents, but was implicated in the scandal nonetheless. Throughout the Supreme Court hearing, he maintained that he was not involved. Interestingly enough, the Army was quick to put out a 'Damocles Sword' over the civilian government by appointing two military officers, Brig (retd) Nauman Saeed (ISI) and Brig Kamran Khurshid (MI) in the Joint Investigation team set up to enquire into the matter at the behest of the Supreme Court.[10]

Even at this beleaguered stage in the build-up to the 2018 elections, Nawaz gave another sensational May 12 interview to Cyril Almeida of the *Dawn* newspaper, berating the running of 'a country...with two or three parallel governments' which, he exhorted, 'had to stop'.

As expected, the Supreme Court disqualified Sharif in July, 2017 from holding public office as he had been dishonest in not disclosing his employment in a Dubai-based company, Capital FZE, in his 2013 election nomination papers. The court also ordered the National Accountability Bureau (NAB) to file a reference against Sharif and his family on corruption charges. A year later, on 6 July 2018, the NAB court sentenced Sharif to ten years in prison along with his daughter, Maryam Nawaz (7 years) and her husband, Safdar Awan (1 year).

The July 2018 elections were held against this backdrop. The military leadership was ensuring that Nawaz Sharif and his PML (N) could not come back to power. Anything but a level playing field was being manipulated, to benefit Imran Khan's Pakistan Tehrik-e-Insaf (PTI). Several feudal 'electable' candidates from South Punjab were made to switch allegiance to Imran Khan's PTI on the promise of making South Punjab a separate province.

Though the PML(N) could win only 85 seats in the 342-member National Assembly compared to the Pakistan Tehrik-e-Insaf (PTI)'s 156 seats, the verdict in the Punjab Provincial Assembly was much closer, with the PML (N) getting 166 seats in the 369-member House against the PTI's 180 seats.[11] With all the controversy surrounding the military's machinations, PML (N) supporters still made a strong show of resistance against the Sharif family arrests. The PML (N)'s hold in central and northern Punjab with its caste and kinship (*biradari*) connections remained intact though Imran Khan's PTI may have been facilitated it to win in several close contests.

Soon after the elections and his arrest in the NAB cases, a personal tragedy befell the ousted PM as his ailing wife, Kulsoom Nawaz, passed away in London (September, 2018) after fighting long against throat cancer.

This was Imran Khan's moment. He had struggled in politics for twenty-two years with single-minded determination to achieve this pinnacle. Not all his tactics were consistent or met his own professed ideological standards. Many were opposed to the PTI's street agitation in 2014, its efforts to get the election results altered or the government ousted by 'extra-constitutional' means. Yet, Imran gave hope to millions of people across a cynical electorate with his agenda of 'Naya Pakistan', promising to rid the country of corruption and working for a compassionate Islamic welfare state focusing on the felt needs of the poor.

Nawaz Sharif was ousted because he fell out with Pakistan's powerful military. Against this backdrop, the Panama cases provided the pretext for his 'legal' disqualification. There was a suspicious money trail. The Sharifs refused to explain their wealth. Their conviction was questionable in the reasoning of the judgments that condemned them and the quality of evidence they were based on. This did not matter in environs where the higher judiciary continued to function as the handmaiden of the military establishment. Throughout Chief Justice Saqib Nisar's tenure, the Supreme Court continued to exercise suo moto jurisdiction in various fields of executive domain. Though the National Accountability Court's judgement in Nawaz Sharif's case was set aside by the Islamabad High Court, the Supreme Judicial Council was prevailed upon to sack Justice Shaukat Siddiqui because he had criticised the ISI.

The 2018 election results provide a temporary respite from chronic civil-military dissonance which has plagued every civilian government in Pakistan. The military wanted a civilian façade and an elected government that would follow its dictates. The outcome suits the army generals to a 'T' with their protégé, Imran, left just short of near majorities, both at the Centre and in Punjab, yet able to form governments, after horse-trading with independents and turncoats. The honeymoon may last as long as Imran does not take any independent foreign policy initiatives, especially pertaining to India, Afghanistan or the USA.

Who after Nawaz?

Against this backdrop, the question about the PML(N)'s political future can have only academic interest for a while. The Army will be in no mood to allow it to resurge unless the Imran Khan government at the centre and his novice protégé in Punjab, CM Usman Buzdar, make a sorry show of handling day-to-day governance. Currently, the PTI seems to be bogged down by the factional squabbling of Punjab feudals such as Pervez Elahi, Speaker, Punjab Assembly and Chaudhry Sarwar, Governor, Punjab, who wait to stab Usman Buzdar in the back the moment he falls from grace of the 'lady kingmaker' and the PM's third wife, 'Lady Bushra Maneka@ ~Pinky Peer'.[12,13] However, the public's patience in regard to indifferent governance can be proverbially long.

Nawaz Sharif's younger brother, Shahbaz Sharif, long-serving Chief Minister of Punjab, Pakistan's largest province with 11 years of experience could have figured in the party's calculations for taking on the premiership after Nawaz if only in the interim. Sixty-five-year-old, Shahbaz had long nursed ambitions to succeed his brother. In Punjab, he built up a good reputation as an efficient administrator credited by bureaucrats as having a longer attention span and a more rigorous working style than his elder sibling. In the past, he, along with Chaudhry Nisar Ali, worked as mediator with the army leadership whenever contentious issues came up in the fraught civil-military relationship.[14] However, Shahbaz's arrest in the alleged Ashiana Housing Scheme (Lahore) scam only re-emphasised the Army's mindset not to allow the Sharif family's political fortunes to revive at this stage. The army leadership was perhaps also making it quite clear that they were ready to dispense with the Sharif family's role in Pakistani politics altogether, if only to enable their new-found protégé, Prime Minister-designate Imran Khan to settle into his new charge.

Earlier, after Nawaz Sharif was forced to quit as PM, 59-year-old Shaheed Khaqan Abbasi, Petroleum Minister in the Nawaz Cabinet in 2017, was appointed interim Prime Minister. An MNA from NA-50 Rawalpindi, he is the son of the Late Khaqan Abbasi, who was Minister in the Junejo Cabinet. Khaqan Abbasi died in the Ojhri ammunition dump explosion of April 1988.

He was a retired Air Commodore, close to the Late President Zia-ul-Haq and despite a rather inglorious role in the Air Force during the 1971 war, was given a sop of an Air Advisor's post in Jordan. Shahid Khaqan completed a Masters in Electrical Engineering from the USA. After that, he did a stint as PIA Chairman (1997-1999) and ran a private airline, Air Blue, since 2007.

Abbasi's candidature as interim PM may have been conditioned by the need to paper over rifts within the ruling party between the Khwaja Asif (Defence Minister) and Chaudhry Nisar Ali (Interior Minister) factions but his lineage spoke of an acceptable defence services connection. His wife is the daughter of a former ISI chief, Maj Gen Muhd Riaz Abbasi (1959-1966) and subsequent Governor of Baluchistan (July 1970 to December 1971). Though Abbasi himself faced allegations of corruption in the past, he is reported to have impressed senior army officers with his acumen during the period he served as acting PM. After initially having been defeated in the July 2018 election from NA-57 Rawalpindi, he won from NA-124 Lahore in a subsequent by-election in October, 2018. He remains a contender for the future leadership of his party in case the Army favours anointing him at a later stage.

Though presently disqualified from politics for ten years due to the Supreme Court's verdict in the Panama case, Maryam Nawaz, daughter of Nawaz Sharif, also remains in contention to resurge at a later stage as the next generation leader of the PML (N). She came into the limelight during the contest for the NA-120 Lahore by-election in January 2018 which she organised in absentia for the ailing Kulsoom Nawaz. Hamza Shahbaz, son of Shahbaz Sharif, had to reluctantly cede ground to Maryam then but he too could re-emerge in the dynasty-ridden politics of the sub-continent if the army's memory of his past actions proves amnesiac.

Before the army leadership gets tired of the PTI, it could also indulge Benazir's son, Bilawal, to emerge in a more positive leadership role to work for the resurgence of the People's Party of Pakistan (PPP).[15] However, the PPP today has a rump presence in Sindh only and any hope for its national resurgence can result only from its revival in Punjab which does not seem a realistic prospect currently.

Meanwhile, the PML (N) retains its kinship (*biradari*) hold in traditional pockets of strength in Punjab and goodwill among the petty bureaucracy it has benefitted over a long sojourn in power during the last two decades.[16,17] It may also hope to benefit in the long run from the factional squabbling of the Punjab feudals in the PTI.

Recently, the Supreme Court (SC) gave bail on medical grounds to Nawaz Sharif. Two curious facts in the developing situation suggest options. First, the more Nawaz defies the military establishment, the more popular he becomes but his political predicament becomes more acute. Nawaz realises perhaps that nothing is permanent in the unstable world of Pakistani politics. Political crises can erupt any time. External factors can have a significant bearing on domestic affairs. Economic necessities can finesse political certainties. This time, his ailing health has added to his troubles. Nawaz could either throw in the towel or continue on the path of defiance. The first route would mean relinquishing control of the PML (N). The second would imply sacrificing his popular legacy. Sharif could be considering a third path. So long as he remains popular with the electorate, so long as his opponents are floundering, so long as the crises of political economy confronting Pakistan continue to expand or deepen, he always has a chance of staging a comeback.[18]

This may or may not be enough to enable the PML (Nawaz) to come back into the Army's favour. Only time will tell.

NOTES

1. S. Akbar Zaidi, Military, *Civil Society and Democratization in Pakistan*, Vanguard Books, Islamabad, 2011, pp. 18.
2. Asad Durrani, *Pakistan Adrift: Navigating Troubled Waters*, C. Hurst & Co., London, 2018.
3. Shuja Nawaz, *Crossed Swords: Pakistan: Its Army, and the Wars Within*, Oxford University Press, Oxford, 2008, pp. 450.
4. Anwar Iqbal, *UPI News*, May 26, 1993.
5. Rana Banerji, "The Military and Nawaz Sharif in Pakistan", Institute of Peace and Conflict Studies, New Delhi, June 5, 2013.
6. Nair Iqbal,"1997 attack on SC: larger bench to hear pleas", *Dawn*, Islamabad, December 5, 2007.
7. Rana Banerji, "The Military and Nawaz Sharif in Pakistan", Institute of Peace and Conflict Studies, New Delhi, June 5, 2013.
8. "Attock Fort: bad memoirs for PMs", *Dawn*, Islamabad, August 27, 2004.
9. International Consortium of Investigative Journalists, April 3, 2016.
10. Hasham Cheema, "How Panama Papers probe unfolded", *Dawn*, Islamabad, April 3, 2016 to July,2018.
11. Election Commission of Pakistan: July 25, 2018: https://ecp.gov.pk/AllResults.aspx
12. Ayesha Siddiqa, "Old men's tales", *The Friday Times*, Lahore, August 17, 2018
13. Arshad Shaheen, "Nisar, Shahbaz call on army chief at GHQ", *Express Tribune*, Karachi, May 26, 2016.
14. The Express Tribune: May 29, 2016, https://tribune.com.pk/story/1112263/national-security-nisar-shahbaz-call-army-chief-ghq/

15. PM Imran, "Bilawal Bhutto attends valima ceremony of COAS Gen. Bajwa's son", *The News*, Karachi, Nov 12, 2018.
16. Anatole Lieven, *Pakistan: A Hard Country*, Penguin UK, London, 2012.
17. Christophe Jaffrelot, *The Pakistan Paradox: Instability and Resilience*, Random House, Gurugram, 2015.
18. Najam Sethi, "Waiting for Godot!", *The Friday Times*, Lahore, March 29, 2019.

8

Pakistan-Significance of Pashtun Protests[1]

Tilak Devasher

Pakistan's capital, Islamabad, has seen many dharnas and protests in the last few years. However, perhaps for the first time, it was witness to a 10-day sit-in (01-10 February 2018) by about 5,000 Pashtuns largely from the Federally Administered Tribal Areas (FATA). The sit-in was an expression of their pent-up feelings of resentment, anger and alienation at their treatment by the state for decades as part of a dubious policy seeking 'strategic depth' in Afghanistan. The import of this event is not merely noteworthy but could well be momentous.

The trigger for the protests was the 13 January 2018 extra-judicial killing of a Pashtun youth, Naqeebullah Mehsud, in Karachi. Naqeebullah hailed from Makeen in South Waziristan in the FATA and belonged to the Abdullahi clan of the Behlolzai sub-tribe, one of the three main branches of the Mehsud tribe.[2] He had migrated with his family to Karachi in the wake of military operations in their hometown. The 23-year-old ran a clothing shop and was an aspiring model. His dance videos and hairstyle had earned him a large Facebook following. He was picked up by plainclothes men on 03 January 2018 and ten days later he was shot dead in a fake encounter. The encounter received nationwide attention for two reasons. First, he did not fit the image of a terrorist from FATA. Second, the police officer involved was the SSP of Karachi's Malir district, Rao Anwar, a known encounter specialist. According to police data, Anwar was in charge of Malir district that has a large Pashtun population from 2011 to 2018. In these seven years he is reported to have 'extra-judicially' killed a staggering 444 people in 200 encounters, a majority of whom were ethnic Pashtuns.

Were it not for the power of social media, Naqeebullah would likely have remained just another statistic passed off as a dead Taliban. With thousands of people taking to the streets in protest, his death became a catalyst in galvanising the Pashtuns on one platform to protest their racial profiling and to seek justice for him. The public outcry from the Pashtun community compelled the government to set up a committee to look into Naqeeb's death. The committee found no evidence of his involvement in terrorism. Hence, his death was established as an extrajudicial murder. Rao Anwar, after failing to flee abroad, has gone underground. If he had been a normal police officer, he would have been arrested by now. The fact that he has not shows that he has connections with the powers-that-be and his arrest and interrogation could open a can of worms.

Naqeebullah's extra-judicial killing proved to be an inflection point. It inspired his fellow tribesmen and other Pashtuns to speak up instead of suffering in silence. The protests began on 18 January when Karachi's Mehsud elders set up a sit-in camp at Sohrab Goth under the banner of the Pashtun Qaumi Jirga. Thousands of people from across the city attended the protest camp. After two weeks, the 'Justice for Naqeeb' movement transformed itself into the 'Pashtun Long March' and shifted to the National Press Club in Islamabad on 01 February. Over 5,000 demonstrators from FATA and other Pashtun areas joined the sit-in. Quick to seize a political opportunity, political leaders from the Pakistan Tehrik-e-Insaf (PTI), Jamiat Ulema-e-Islam-Fazl (JUI-F), Pakhtunkhwa Milli Awami Party (PkMAP) and Awami National Party (ANP) expressed support for the protestors.

What had begun as a demand for the arrest of Rao Anwar soon evolved into a comprehensive set of specific demands. They included: (i) the immediate arrest and prosecution of Rao Anwar; (ii) stopping of enforced disappearances and extrajudicial killings across Pakistan and their investigation; (iii) an end to the harassment and humiliation of the people of the tribal areas; and, (iv) the removal of all landmines from FATA that had injured or killed a large number of people. The sit-in was called off after 10 days on 10 February after the government gave a written assurance that former SSP Rao Anwar would soon be apprehended and the genuine grievances raised by protestors would be addressed as soon as possible. The organisers insist that this is a temporary halt for a month and that the resistance would continue if the government did not implement their promises.

A remarkable feature of the protest was that it was completely peaceful and the protesters issued no threats. This was in marked contrast to the blasphemy protests carried out at the Faizabad interchange in November 2017. The resonance of the protests was such that even Afghan President Ghani (a Pashtun) tweeted that he fully supported the historical #PashtunLongMarch in Pakistan. He termed the protests a "wake-up call against fundamentalism".[3]

In the name of fighting terror, the Pak army has carried out several operations in FATA during the last decade, especially targeting North and South Waziristan. In such operations, over 2 million people have been displaced and have had to move into camps or seek refuge in urban centres of Pakistan. The army has treated these areas as war zones and launched a full-fledged war on its own population. Measures taken include planting land mines, imposing blanket curfews and erecting pervasive check posts all over FATA. Continuation of such measures either negates the claim of completely driving out the terrorists from the region or is a cover for some harsh realities.

The harsh reality is that the Pashtuns have been used as cannon fodder by the state for the sake of its exaggerated geo-strategic objectives. Their territory became the safe haven for terrorists that were nurtured by the state over the decades. Consequently, the Pashtuns have been subjected to a war not of their making for the past three decades with horrendous violence against their lives and properties. They have been displaced from their homes and face almost daily insults and humiliation. While the conditions in FATA are pitiable (70 per cent of the five million population lives in poverty), the condition of Pashtuns in the urban centres is no better. It is undeniable that Pashtuns in general and especially those from FATA have been negatively stereotyped and looked at with suspicion for years in almost all urban centres. The issue, as a human rights activist, Jibran Nasir, puts it 'is about racial profiling.'[4] There are many examples of profiling of Pashtuns as terrorists. For one thing, in the name of fighting terror, thousands of young Pashtun boys have been picked up and have just disappeared in the last decade and a half. Last year, the Punjab police specifically targeted the Pashtun community in Lahore and Rawalpindi as suspects of terrorism. More recently, after clashes between student unions in Punjab University the police jailed almost 200 Pashtun and Baloch students on charges of terrorism. A Pashtun senator charged that the students were being treated as if they were prisoners of war or belonged to a foreign country and faced acute racial discrimination while the Punjab Government, its police and opposition looked the other way.[5] Another example is of a book on Pakistan studies being taught in Punjab that contains abusive and insulting words like traitors and illiterate for Pashtuns.

Not surprisingly, Pashtun alienation is running high. According to Dr Said Alam Mehsud, a rights activist, 'Being Pashtun is now sin in this country.'[6,7]

Pakistan often cites the figure of 60,000 Pakistani civilians killed in the war of terror but never reveals the ethnic composition of those killed. It is believed that at least 95 per cent of them would be Pashtuns. There is now a growing anger among the Pashtun youth at how they have been sacrificed at the altar of distant foreign policy goals. They don't want to be sacrificial lambs any more. Young Pashtuns who have been studying in the urban centres of Pakistan, especially Karachi and Lahore, have personally experienced ethnic profiling and discrimination. This has led to the emergence of a political consciousness that is questioning the way the community has been treated all these years. For them, the frame of reference is not the old nationalist thinking but actual ground-level experiences of Pashtuns in today's Pakistan. These experiences include displacement from their homes, ethnic profiling, being subjected to unlawful abductions, detentions, torture and killings by security forces on the one hand and terrorist violence and drone attacks, on the other.

The Islamabad sit-in is perhaps the first sign of the growth of this new political consciousness whose message clearly is that Pashtun lives are not expendable. In a sense, the protests have rekindled the issue of Pashtun identity that was thought by many to have been co-opted and submerged in a larger Pakistan identity. The moot point is not whether the government implements the demands or whether the protest gets translated into a sustained political movement that can effectively address longstanding structural issues. The moot point is that the protests have raised the question of what it means to be a Pashtun in 21st-century Pakistan.[8] By doing so, the protests have redefined Pashtun political discourse in Pakistan.[9]

The Pashtun anger and outrage is real and if ignored or treated lightly could become dangerous. As '*The Nation*' warned, "If the government fails to cater the demands of the tribal people, the chances are that the militancy will take up the form of militant ethnic nationalism."[10] Naqeebullah's murder has ensured that the Pakistan state has to face the reality of Pashtun alienation and can no longer treat them as cannon fodder. What impact, if any, this has on the policies of the state will have to be carefully watched.

NOTES

1. First published by VIF on 05 March 2018, https://www.vifindia.org/article/2018/march/05/pakistan-significance-of-pashtun-protests
2. Rahimullah Yusufzai, 'Mehsuds struggle to find a voice', The News, 11 February 2018.
3. Staff Reporter, "Afghan president backs Islamabad sit-in", Dawn, Islamabad. February 10, 2018.
4. Syed Raza Hassan, "Pakistan Police Killing of Pashtun Youth Fuels anger over 'Encounters'", Reuters, London, January 27, 2018.
5. Mumtaz Alvi, "Issue of violence against Pakhtun, Baloch students in Lahore echoes in Senate", The News, Karachi, January 27, 2018.
6. Abdur Rauf Yousafzai, "Long march against Naqeeb killing reaches Peshawar", Daily Times, Lahore, January 29, 2018.
7. Aslam Kakar, "The problem with 'terrorism' charges'", Daily Times, Lahore, February 7, 2018.
8. Rafiullah Kakar, "Pashtun sit-in—a new political awakening?" The Express Tribune, Karachi, February 8, 2018.
9. Afrasiab Khattak, "Pashtun protest", The Nation, Lahore, February 10, 2018.
10. "Pashtun Sit-In Ends", The Nation, Lahore, February 12, 2018.

9

The Pakistan Tahafuz Movement (PTM): One Year Later

Tilak Devasher

The Pashtun Tahafuz Movement (PTM) has taken the Pashtun[1] belt in Pakistan by storm as also the Pashtun Diaspora in several countries. In the one year of its existence, the PTM has become a broad-based movement challenging the state's attitude towards the Pashtuns, especially in the former Federally Administered Tribal Areas (FATA) during the anti-terror operations. Apart from the sheer size of its gatherings, the participation of women in the conservative Pashtun society has been remarkable. Its activities in the past year have shown that it was not a temporary outpouring of anger and frustration in a war-ravaged region. Instead, 'the PTM has come to represent a resilient, peaceful and popular initiative that has withstood extensive state repression, persecution and a media blackout since its inception.'[2] What distinguishes the PTM from previous movements is that it has resolutely protested state policies that have imposed an armed conflict on the Pashtuns.

The Beginnings[3]

The PTM originated in the Mehsud Tahafuz Movement (MTM) that was begun in May 2014 by eight students at Gomal University, Dera Ismail Khan. The objective of the initiative was to push for the removal of landmines from the Mehsud area in Waziristan. What transformed the MTM into the PTM was the extra-judicial killing of Naqeebullah Mehsud in a fake police encounter led by SSP Rao Anwar in Karachi in January 2018. His killing prompted the Pashtun 'long march' from Dera Ismail Khan to Islamabad in February 2018 that soon became the rallying cry for the community that had had enough of the war and the displacement that it entailed due to the state's Afghan policy.

What has sustained the PTM was the manner in which Anwar's case was treated making a mockery of the criminal justice system. His demeanour in court, his arrival with full protocol and without handcuffs, his confinement for a few months in his own home that was declared a sub-jail and his getting bail from an anti-terrorism court were all indicative that the state was not really serious about his prosecution. A year later, the trial court has yet to indict Rao Anwar (who has since retired from service) or the other 25 suspects. As has been pointed out, 'The message that the lack of a trial thus far in the Naqeebullah case and the shocking indulgence shown to the prime suspect is that the police need fear no consequences for their actions against a hostage citizenry.'[4]

Manzoor Pashteen, a 24-year-old (in 2018) Mehsud Pashtun, has emerged as the leader of the movement. His family had been displaced from their home in South Waziristan in 2009 when he was in high school and they were forced to seek refuge in Dera Ismail Khan. Initially, his efforts were focussed towards helping his Mehsud tribe, among the worst victims in Pakistan's war on terror both in terms of lives lost, property damaged and the fact that they were forced to flee their homeland. According to Pashteen, 'The extremism was deliberately imposed here. The war fought here in the name of terrorism was fake because both sides terrorized civilians. The change now is that such traumatized people are determined to gain all the rights that the [Pakistani] constitution grants them, but they also want accountability for what happened to them.'[5]

In an article published in the *New York Times*, Pashteen wrote: '...our economic and political rights, and our suffering have remained invisible to most of Pakistan and the world because the region was seen as a dangerous frontier after numerous militants moved there after the fall of the Taliban. The government ignored us when these militants terrorized and murdered the residents. Pakistan's military operations against the militants brought further misery: civilian killings, displacements, enforced disappearances, humiliation and the destruction of our livelihoods and way of life. No journalists were allowed into the tribal areas while the military operations were going on. Pashtuns who fled the region in hopes of rebuilding their lives in Pakistani cities were greeted with suspicion and hostility. We were stereotyped as terrorist sympathizers. I was studying to become a veterinarian, but the plight of my people forced me and several friends to become activists.'[6]

It was Pashteen who, together with 20 friends, had set out on a 'long march' from Dera Ismail Khan through the Peshawar valley, the Pashtun heartland, to Islamabad in the first week of February 2018 that led to the transformation of the MTM into the PTM.

Rise and Growth of the PTM

Several factors account for the stunning popularity and mobilisation of the PTM.

One reason has been the apathy of mainstream Pakistani political parties towards the plight of the Pashtuns due to their compromises with the army for loaves of office. The persisting cycles of wars in and for Afghanistan have brought the Pashtuns the three Ds: 'death, destruction, and displacement'[7] leading to anger among the Pashtuns welling up over decades. However, the political parties, especially the Awami National Party (ANP), did very little to assuage the misery of the Pashtuns. This was largely due to the transformation of the ANP from a party representing Pashtun nationalism to becoming a mainstream party. In the process, it chose not to articulate wider Pashtun grievances wrought about by the effects of the war on terror. It thus diluted its mass resistance-based politics and instead adopted policies of seeking accommodation with the army for electoral victories. As a result, a gulf developed between Pashtun political grievances and consciousness and the ANP. This gulf has been increasingly filled by the PTM with its rights-based, non-parliamentary agenda that has fired the imagination of the Pashtun masses as well as of the whole country.

A second reason has been the plight of the Internally Displaced Persons (IDPs). Operation Zarb-e-Azab that was launched in 2014 led some one million residents of North Waziristan to flee their homes for more than three years. Even when some of them returned, they had to contend with destroyed homes and deserted villages; rehabilitation was tardy. As one scribe put it: 'Projects funded by multi-donor trusts are not taking off, so there is no chance of more funds being allocated for existing projects, or of new projects being undertaken.'[8] Even the Benazir Income Support Programme is not extended to North and South Waziristan.

Moreover, rather than being rehabilitated with some dignity, they were forced to take a new oath of allegiance to the state and carry special 'Watan

Cards' that were sarcastically referred to as visas to their home towns. It was left to Gen Qamar Javed Bajwa, the army chief, to abolish them. Living in refugee camps and in Pakistan's urban centres, the IDPs faced humiliation being viewed as terrorists or facilitators. The extra-judicial killing of Naqibullah Mehsud is but one example of this attitude. The mainstream media, both print and electronic, as also political parties failed to project the plight of the IDPs that aggravated their angst. This collective anguish, neglect and humiliation ultimately led to the PTM coming to the fore and providing a platform to all those affected by the military operation.

Third, what has provided new adherents is the fact that after every major peaceful protest, the police has been arresting and charging PTM activists and supporters with rioting, treason or terrorism, further fuelling Pashtun anger. As Pashteen wrote in an article, their activists, especially women, faced relentless online harassment while social media posts expressing support for PTM campaigns led to a knock from the intelligence services. Many of their supporters were fired from their jobs; many have been held under terrorism laws.[9] However, the effort of the state to silence the movement using official harassment has not been successful. On the contrary, the PTM has actually gained greater traction with its rallies attracting larger crowds signalling that it is going nowhere no matter how hard the government tries to sweep it under the rug.

Fourth, the media has ignored Pashtun protests from day one with most journalists choosing to exercise self-censorship. For example, while the Pak media on 5 February 2019 beamed live the banned Jamat-ud-Dawa (JuD) led Kashmir Day protest outside the Press Club in Islamabad, it blanked out the police crackdown on a peaceful PTM protest in the same area. Politicians and experts kept delivering traditional statements on Kashmir, but none spoke of the human rights abuse happening under their noses by their own government. As Ilyas Khan of the *BBC* wrote, it is "a protest Pakistan wants to hide from the world."[10] However, blocking coverage by the mainstream media has not been very effective due to the social media. If anything, the movement has caught international attention largely due to the reporting of its activities on the social media. Attempts to suppress the protests have only widened alienation.[11]

In a signed article in the *New York Times* published on 11 February 2019, Manzoor Pashteen wrote that vile propaganda against the PTM was reported as news while the security establishment ensured that almost nothing was reported about their movement in the mainstream Pakistani newspapers and television networks. The military had unleashed thousands of trolls to run a disinformation campaign against the PTM accusing it of starting a "hybrid war." They were accused almost daily of conspiring with Indian, Afghan or American intelligence services. [12]

Another element in the situation has been the slow, if not non-existent, implementation of legal and administrative reforms that had to be done after FATA was merged into Khyber Pakhtunkhwa (KPK) in 2018. The FATA Interim Governance Regulation 2018 dated 28 May 2018 replaced the draconian Frontier Crimes Regulations (FCR) and outlined how FATA would be governed, "within a timeframe of two years", while the region was merged with the KPK.[13] Resultantly, more than six million Pashtun residents of these areas are in 'legal limbo and an administrative vacuum.' The army is running the day-to-day administration. One consequence of this is that voices are invariably raised against the army simply because there is no civilian institution that can be the focus of people's anger.[14]

Activities

The PTM has kept up the tempo of its activities during the past year. After the Islamabad protests in February 2018, it has organised protest rallies in major cities including Quetta, Peshawar, Lahore, Karachi and in smaller cities like Swat, Dera Ismail Khan, Swabi and Bannu. On 13 January 2019 it held a rally in Tank to observe the first anniversary of the killing of Naqeebullah Mehsud. What is touching at these rallies is that thousands of men, women and children hold aloft photos and tattered birth certificates from their missing relatives hoping that the PTM can somehow reunite them with their loved ones.

There have been at least two efforts at engaging mainstream politicians. A PTM delegation led by PTM leader and MNA Mohsin Dawar met Pakistan Peoples Party (PPP) chairman Bilawal Bhutto-Zardari and his father and former president Asif Ali Zardari in Islamabad on 30 April 2019. Later, Zardari said that the demands of the PTM were justified and a dialogue should be held with their leadership. Interestingly, in response to a question about the ISPR chief's statement that the game was over for the PTM, the former president said cryptically the "game never ends".[15]

On another occasion, a special committee of senators headed by Senator Barrister Mohammad Ali Saif of the Mohajir Qaumi Movement (MQM) invited the PTM leaders for a hearing on their complaints. The special committee was formed to "examine purported grievances amongst some sections of the society and reach out/engage with the genuinely aggrieved persons to create national cohesion." After a three-hour session with the PTM leadership on 16 April 2019, the committee asked it to nominate a focal person for effective coordination and to present its demands in writing in order to suggest a workable solution after consultation with all stakeholders. According to an official hand-out issued by the Senate Secretariat after the meeting, the PTM chief Pashteen said: "Measures must be taken for resolving the issue of missing persons, demining of the landmines and for constitution of a Truth and Reconciliation Commission to restore the confidence of the people of the [tribal] area."[16] The event was hailed as historic and the need was stressed for a continuing dialogue.

The PTM has not been impressed with Imran Khan who despite boasting Pashtun origins has chosen to do little to change the state's attitude toward their demands for justice and civil rights. He has made at least two references to the PTM in his public speeches. Speaking at a public gathering in Kalaya, the headquarters of Orakzai tribal district on 19 April 2019, Imran Khan made a reassuring speech that was a clear conciliation offer—an olive branch held out to the PTM agreeing to its grievances that the Pashtuns had paid and continued to pay the price for militancy that plagued the tribal regions.[17] He thus accepted that the concerns and issues of the PTM were legitimate ones, though he was critical of the tone and tenor they were using. He added that the issues being highlighted by the PTM now were the same he had spoken about 15 years ago.[18]

Addressing another gathering on 24 April in Wana, Imran Khan, in a veiled reference to the PTM, said some elements operating in the region have been receiving money from abroad to push the youth of the tribal districts towards unrest. He added that such elements had been trying to cash in on the problems being faced by locals.[19] In this second speech, his narrative closely approximated that of the army.

Most movements have evocative slogans to motivate their followers and provide an identity. In the case of the PTM, three such slogans have come to the fore so far. The first was: "*Yeh jo dehshatgardi hai, is ke peechay wardi hai*" (behind this terrorism, is the [military] uniform). This openly pointed to a nexus between the terrorists and the army. The slogan questioned the inability of the army to eliminate terrorism from FATA if it really wanted to do so. The second is "*Da Sang Azadi Da?*" (What kind of freedom is this?) that is the punch line of the PTM's anthem. Its latest slogan—*lar-o-bar yaw Afghan?* [People of] (low and highlands are one Afghan) has been interpreted by the army as indicative of secessionist intentions—the spectre of merging of Pakistani Pashtun (*Lar*) with their Afghan brethren (*Bar*) in the so-called Greater Afghanistan.

These slogans certainly have been perceived to be anti-state and anti-army.[20] Resultantly, Pakistan leaders, especially the army, have been getting nightmares about the Pashtun nationalist narrative that has looked upon the Durand Line as an imposed colonial boundary dividing Pashtuns into two states.

Slogans apart, another powerful symbol of the movement is the distinctive, embroidered red-and-black Mazari cap. Manzoor Pashteen had apparently exchanged this headgear with a tribal for the one off his own head. Such has been the power and resonance of this symbol that similar caps have been banned from several places, including the Bannu University that called the wearing of this specific cap 'subversive' and a sign of ethnic divide.[21]

Demands

When it started out in February 2018, the main demands of the PTM were (i) the immediate arrest and prosecution of Rao Anwar; (ii) stopping of enforced disappearances and extrajudicial killings and their investigation; (iii) an end to the harassment and humiliation of the people of the tribal areas; and (iv) the removal of all landmines from FATA. Over the past year, other demands have been added. For example, at a rally of about 30,000 people at Miranshah in April 2019, Manzoor Pashteen raised a new element when he said: "...we are sons of this soil and we want to have a complete hold on the resources of this soil; otherwise no one can stop us from getting our rights and hold on our resources." He added that the resources of Pashtuns had been stolen and captured by others and now it was time for them to stand up and get equal rights from this state.[22] He said there was a plan to extract these resources and transport them to the Punjab, as had been done in the past and that their killing and the destruction of their wealth amounted to a systematic campaign to subjugate the Pashtuns.[23]

Asking for resources is an interesting element in the PTM narrative. The key resource of KPK is water, something that is becoming increasingly scarce in Pakistan.

Nature of the PTM

The unique thing about the PTM is that perhaps for the first time in Pakistan someone has challenged the holiest of holies—the army for enforcing, in letter and spirit, rights under the constitution. This belief of the army trampling their fundamental rights as enshrined in the constitution is based on personal experiences of devastation wrought about by the army's policies. Not surprisingly, the PTM has across-the-board acceptability among the Pashtuns.

Second, the PTM is the latest phenomenon in the history of non-violent protests among the Pashtuns. For example, the Khudai Khidmatgars remained non-violent despite the 1930 massacre at Qissa Khwani and again the 1948 killing at Babara in Charsadda. Qayyum Khan, the then chief minister of the North-Western Frontier Province (NWFP—today KPK) had ordered the latter. He later boasted that the Khudai Khidmatgars were lucky that the police ran out of ammunition; "otherwise, not a single soul would have survived." Similarly, ANP leaders Mian Iftikhar Hussain and the late Bashir Bilour stood up to the Taliban and drew their inspiration from Qissa Khwani and Babara. Their historic words were that "your bullets and bombs will run out, but not our chests." One of them laid down his life and another lost his only son but they remain undeterred. Despite the PTM being a peaceful movement, the growing perception among the Pashtuns is that violence by the army is a deliberate attempt to provoke violent responses.[24]

Third, it is led largely by the youth who were born and grew up during war on terror. The youth have personal experience of the army helping Taliban factions to control parts of Waziristan and how these factions, in the name of *Aman*, or peace committees, had terrorized the local population. These committees even performed key functions of the state, ran parallel courts and meted out punishments despite the presence of thousands of Pak troops who were largely confined to camps. The civilians could not complain to anyone.

Fourth, the PTM draws its ideological and political support from the two mainstream Pashtun parties—the Awami National Party (ANP) and the Pashtunkhwa Milli Awami Party (PkMAP). However, the PTM has gone further and raised new contemporary issues that these parties had chosen to underplay due to compulsions of electoral politics and power sharing.[25] Not surprisingly, the ANP especially has felt threatened because the PTM has challenged its monopoly over Pashtun nationalism.

Fifth, the international gatherings of the PTM seem to be attracting many who have an anti-Pakistan agenda. In such meetings, PTM supporters have openly threatened the state and the army; Pashtuns in KPK have been incited to revolt and join Afghanistan; racist language has been used against Punjab. The PTM has not distanced itself from the anti-Pakistani elements abroad. In fact, such meetings, of late, have been addressed by Manzoor Pashteen.[26] Such signals have reinforced the suspicion in the army that the PTM is a potential threat to the integrity of Pakistan.

Impact

Perhaps the most important impact of the PTM is that it has been successful in breaking the circle of fear in KPK, especially in its western districts (formally known as FATA) that had forced people to suffer atrocities silently. Prior to the emergence of the PTM, local resistance to the Taliban or against the excesses of the army failed because some of the protestors were killed and the others frightened into submission. What the PTM has done is to unite the population and to protest unitedly. The movement has given a voice to the suffering people who had been at the receiving end of extremist violence and state oppression. Now they have a platform where they can openly speak about their sufferings caused by both the Taliban and the army. Resultantly, generations of Pashtuns have been coming forward to narrate their stories. A common thread are lives traumatized by missing fathers, brothers and sons, of surviving for years dealing with terrorists first and then with the army and how they were regarded with suspicion and hostility living as refugees within their own country. According to Pashteen, activism has created awareness that the Pashtuns were mere pawns in a war that was fought for the benefit and interests of others in which there was collusion between the military and the militants, particularly pro-government and surrendered Taliban. The people were now unwilling to accept or tolerate any militants or Taliban.[27]

Independent observers have corroborated these stories and confirmed that during the 'clearance' operations in the tribal areas there was widespread abuse of authority and use of force. That led to massive damage to properties and loss of lives of innocent civilians.

According to noted journalist Gul Bukhari, PTM protests encouraged a tribal Wazir woman to come out in the open about sexual harassment at the hands of the Pakistani military. This was unprecedented 'because honour prevented men and women of the tribal areas from speaking about dishonour of womenfolk.' A video of a Wazir child from Mir Ali, North Waziristan, alleging repeated sexual harassment of the female members of his household at the hands of army officers (all elder males had been taken away by the security forces) went viral on social media provoking national outrage and PTM protests. When the charge was denied, the woman, encouraged by the PTM's support, repeated her son's claims in a video from behind the traditional burqa.[28]

One immediate impact of the PTM protests was that the state was forced to conduct an inquiry that found circumstantial evidence of Rao Anwar's presence at the scene of the killing of Naqeebullah Mehsud. He was accused of registering fake criminal cases, kidnapping, murder and destroying evidence. While it is true that the trial of Rao Anwar is going nowhere, the fact is that he was suspended and put on trial. Previously he had 'encountered' over 400 Pakistanis in fake police encounters but none of them had resulted in state action against him. It was the pressure of the Pashtun protests that forced the state to put him on trial.

Two other positive results of the PTM agitation have been that the army has been forced to relax the stringent security measures at checkpoints where civilians had to wait for hours and the special biometric IDs for Waziristan residents, the Watan Card, that Waziristan residents had to carry to travel have been discarded. Another success of the PTM is that the authorities have begun to release persons who had earlier disappeared and against whom they had no substantial evidence.

Recent Developments

While the extra-judicial killing of Naqeebullah Mehsud was the catalyst that provoked the PTM, the movement has been sustained with continuing killings. Prof Arman Loni was one of the leaders of the PTM who was arrested after returning from a sit-in protest outside Loralai Press Club in Baluchistan on 2 February 2019. The sit-in protest had been staged against a recent terror attack. Pakistani media reports stated Loni had been sitting in a park after the protest when police arrested him. He later died in police custody. Over two dozen PTM activists were arrested in Islamabad when they gathered to protest the death of Arman Loni. For over 24 hours, the whereabouts of one detainee, prominent rights activist Gulalai Ismail, recipient of the International Humanist of the Year Award, was unknown to her family and legal counsel.[29] Prominent human rights activist and Professor Dr. Ammar Ali Jan was arrested from his residence in the early hours of the morning. There is no evidence that any of those detained or arrested were indulging in activities against the State; rather they were peacefully demonstrating.[30] Another case was the abduction and brutal murder of Tahir Dawar, a decorated police officer from Waziristan. This remains un-investigated despite official promises at the highest level.

The death of Arman Luni could be an important and dangerous moment in Pakistan's history. For the Pashtuns, the contrast between how the media and the nation reacted to the death of a Pashtun at the hands of security officials and that of a Punjabi in Sahiwal in Punjab,[31] angered the community and led them to ask whether they were not equal citizens? The primary reason that the Sahiwal incident was highlighted in the mainstream and social media was that it occurred in Punjab.

Thirteen activists of the PTM were killed on 26 May 2019 when the army opened fire on a large group of protesters in North Waziristan. The army, on the other hand, claims that PTM members attacked a military checkpoint and wounded security forces before any shooting began in which three activists were shot dead. The army has, however, shown no evidence to counter witness accounts and videos largely pointing to the contrary. The PTM denied attacking the checkpost and videos on social media support its claim. Using this as an excuse, the army, however, arrested two of its leaders, MNAs Ali Wazir and Mohsin Dawar. At the time of writing, they continue to be under detention and were not even allowed to attend parliament sessions.

All these cases have further added fuel to the fire of alienation.

Response of the Army

The army was caught off-guard when the movement emerged in February 2018. Its initial response seemed to be to accept the PTM's lesser demands by relaxing curfews, ending aggressive searches on check posts and launching a demining program in Waziristan. By April 2018, hundreds of disappeared Pashtuns, mostly in military custody, were released.

However, by mid-April, the army began having second thoughts. 'No anti-state agenda would be allowed under the garb of those protests,' Army Chief General Qamar Javed Bajwa said on 12 April 2018. In what would become the military's standard narrative, Bajwa soon linked the PTM to a hybrid war aimed at weakening Pakistan internally. "Our enemies know they cannot beat us fair and square and have thus subjected us to a cruel, evil, and protracted hybrid war. They are trying to weaken our resolve by weakening us from within," he told newly-graduated officers on 14 April 2018.[32]

The army's ambivalent attitude towards the PTM was evident in June 2018 when former Taliban members, whom officials called a 'peace' committee, killed several unarmed PTM protesters. On cue, the military made its views clear. As the DG ISPR said on 4 June, "We solved their problems, but how then is there still a campaign on social media? How were 5,000 social media accounts created in Afghanistan in a single day, and how was a cap made outside the country and imported into Pakistan [to become the symbol of the PTM]?" Tellingly, he defended the Taliban 'peace' committee claiming that they fought in the war against terrorism for years.[33]

The army has been floundering on how to deal with this political phenomenon because it has shown none of the weaknesses of traditional movements that could be exploited; its leadership is young and without baggage of the past; its narrative is not based on hearsay but on personal experiences of destruction and humiliation. As a result, the normal policies of carrot-and-stick have not worked. What the army has not been able to countenance is the fact that the PTM narrative is centred on the army, as an institution, using the Pashtuns for foreign policy objectives. As evidence, they cite the fact that almost all the demands of the PTM essentially relate to the army. Hence, the army's conclusion is that the real agenda of the PTM is to malign and defame the army by exploiting the sufferings of the displaced Pashtuns.

For the army, by articulating ethnic rights, the PTM has crossed its red line, suffering as it continues to do from the Bangladesh syndrome. It has issued several public warnings in this regard and also tried to curb its activities in the only manner it knows. The army's muscular tactics have included heavy censorship of their activities, smear campaigns, obstructing and harassing leaders, activists and supporters of the movement, preventing leaders from entering parts of Pakistan where they wanted to hold rallies, preventing leaders from travelling abroad by putting them on the exit control list, detention for weeks, enforced disappearances, alongside the use of brute force. Other dirty tricks include denying permission for gatherings or strewing garbage and flooding the venue with sewer water as was done at the movement's Lahore rally in 2018. However, the organisers were able to overcome this with an effective communications network and efficient volunteers to pump out the water and clean the venue. During a function in London, one of the state elements even set off the fire alarm that disrupted the PTM meeting.[34]

In early January 2019, Major General Asif Ghafoor, DG Inter-Services Public Relations (ISPR), reached out to the PTM and asked its members to work with the army to help fulfil the PTM's demands.³⁵ A change in the tack of the ISPR was apparent during a guided tour for local and foreign media persons it had organised to Miramshah towards the end of January 2019. Three points were emphasised: the PTM was the critical factor hampering the trust-building process between the military and local community; the PTM was negatively affecting the morale of the security forces deployed in the region; the PTM factor was opening up space for the Tehreek-Taliban Pakistan (TTP).³⁶ A narrative that the army seems to be developing was to label the PTM and the Taliban "two faces of the same coin," Thus, in an April 2019 press conference, the DG ISPR accused the PTM of being in cahoots with the TTP since they both had an identical narrative.

On 26 April 2019, DG ISPR held a press conference in which the army finally made it clear that the PTM's 'time was up'. His press conference was one of the most hard-hitting statements against the PTM by the military till then, going far beyond the crossing 'red-lines' assertions. The DG ISPR accused the PTM of receiving funds from the intelligence agencies of India and Afghanistan to pursue its campaign in Pakistan and even beyond. Apart from foreign funding, DG ISPR highlighted another concern: the language used by the PTM during its protest demonstrations. He claimed that the army had addressed several concerns of the PTM but was disappointed with the continuing bitterness of the PTM rhetoric and the anti-army slogans raised at PTM rallies.³⁷

The spokesman indicated that the law would take its course against PTM leaders. However, he did not elaborate the action contemplated but clarified that his statement should not be construed as a "declaration of war" against the group and nothing "illegal would be done" nor would inconvenience be caused to ordinary Pashtuns who were being incited by PTM leaders. According to him, 45 per cent of the mined area had been cleared at the cost of 101 military casualties, the number of checkpoints had decreased and the number of missing persons had dropped to 2,500. On missing persons, the military spokesman reminisced about the security situation through which the country passed and said: "We don't want anyone to be missing, but war is ruthless." He then added ominously, 'Everything is fair in love and war."³⁸ He said the Inquiry Commission on Enforced Disappearances had shortened the list of missing persons from 8,000 to 2,500 cases. He mischievously asked the PTM to share the list of manpower of TTP that was sitting in Afghanistan as well as other insurgent groups so that he could tally it to see if any missing person was actually sitting there.³⁹

Possibly the army had concluded that its hands-off approach had strengthened the PTM and emboldened it to indulge in seditious activities. The nature of the 'iron hand' that the army would adopt against the peaceful movement unfolded in May 2019 with the killing of unarmed PTM protesters and arrest of MNA Ali Wazir and later MNA Mohsin Dawar, mentioned earlier.

In Pakistan, the army has appropriated the monopoly of declaring who is patriotic and who are traitors and fifth columnists. Thus, the PTM is now in distinguished company of Pak nationals who the army has decreed to be traitors and foreign agents. The list includes luminaries like Fatima Jinnah, the sister of Quaid-i-Azam, Huseyn Suhrawardy, a former prime minister of Pakistan, and G.M. Syed, who had moved the Pakistan Resolution in the Sindh Assembly[40] and, in more recent times, Benazir Bhutto and Nawaz Sharif.

However, by labelling the PTM as a national security threat, what the army has done is to reduce the space for the civilian government for taking any initiative to resolve the issues raised. As a commentator put it, 'The establishment would probably find it easier to engage with rights-based movements if they had a religious agenda.'[41]

Afghanistan

The Afghans have been keeping a close watch on the developments relating to the PTM. The Afghans, especially the Afghan Pashtuns, are acutely aware how Pakistan, working through its Taliban proxies, has wreaked havoc, death and destruction in Afghanistan. The anti-war narrative of the PTM has thus resonated with the Pashtuns in Afghanistan who are equally tired of Taliban violence supported and fomented by Pakistan. There is common suffering on both sides of the Durand Line that brings the Pashtuns across the Pak-Afghan border on the same page that the *lar-o-bar* slogan underlines.

When the Pashtun long march began it did not escape notice in Afghanistan. Afghan President Ashraf Ghani (a Pashtun) tweeted in February 2018 that he fully supported the historical #PashtunLongMarch in Pakistan, the main purpose of which was to mobilize citizens against fundamentalism and terrorism in the region. He termed the protests a "wake-up call against fundamentalism."[42] Once again he tweeted on 7 February 2019: "The Afghan government has serious concerns about the violence perpetrated against peaceful protestors and civil activists in Khyber Pakhtunkhwa and Balochistan."[43] Ghani's tweets have been perceived as having far greater geopolitical implications than just merely extending support to the Pashtuns. They have been viewed as stoking Pashtun sentiments against Pakistan.[44]

Apart from Ghani's tweet, several protests were held in Afghanistan to condemn the killing of the PTM members. In a recent development, a group of young activists from Bamiyan province, the centre of Afghanistan, gathered in front of the Buddhas of Bamiyan and called for their support to the PTM members.[45]

The Road Ahead

As the PTM has grown and become larger, it is faced with the issue of evolving from just being a pressure group representing Pashtun angst, especially of the youth, into thinking about long-term goals. For this, it will have to make crucial decisions about structures, policies and socio-political goals.[46] One such issue is the debate about whether it should pursue parliamentary politics or remain a mass resistance movement. Two PTM leaders, Ali Wazir and Mohsin Dawar, contested and won parliamentary elections in July 2018 but as independent candidates. They have raised issues pertaining to rights guaranteed under the constitution in the National Assembly that traditional politicians have not raised earlier.

Two of the demands of the PTM—extrajudicial killings and forced disappearances—affect other nationalities like the Mohajirs in Karachi, Sindhi nationalists, Baloch and even some Punjabis. Not surprisingly, during the past year, the PTM has begun to attract the support of these other ethnic groups who have been equally the victims of forced disappearances for years. A moot point is whether the PTM would be able to form an alliance with the other smaller ethnicities of Pakistan who too have suffered and are suffering at the hands of the security agencies. As journalist Gul Bukhari wrote: 'PTM is no longer just about the Pashtuns. In the past year, this extraordinarily brave and non-violent movement has brought into its fold the support of disaffected Sindhis, Mohajirs and the Baloch, who have also suffered enforced disappearances for decades.'[47] Jointly, these oppressed nationalities may be able to generate greater pressure than singly to ensure that the agencies act within the bounds of the law.

Conclusion

The two main strengths of the PTM are its non-violent character and its broad-based support from almost all segments of Pashtun society.[48] There are genuine reasons for anger and alienation among the Pashtuns who have been at the receiving end during four decades of constant warfare coupled with negligence and apathy of the state. Instead of focusing on these basic issues, the army has tried to divert attention by alleging the role of a foreign hand behind the rise and growth of the PTM and prevented it from getting media attention. Such moves are proving to be counterproductive and will increase the frustration of an already alienated generation.

The moot question that is being raised is why does the state regard a peaceful Pashtun rights movement as an enemy conspiracy rather than what it is—a movement of Pakistanis demanding their rights and asking for justice? Like the Baloch, the Bengalis, and the Sindhis before them, the Pashtuns are increasingly coming to believe that in Pakistan, non-Punjabis do not have the right to seek justice and make their voices heard.[49] Such a belief, if it continues to grow, could have dangerous portents for Pakistan.

Can the PTM escalate into a secessionist movement? At the moment, the chances of this happening are low for several reasons. For one, Pashtuns are well integrated into Pakistan. For another, there are better facilities for education, economy and livelihood for the Pashtuns in Pakistan than in Afghanistan. Third, the Pashtuns in Pakistan as yet do not have real issue with Punjab that would motivate racism or violence against it.

However, the danger is that if coercive action is taken against the already alienated Pashtuns, there could be a more severe reaction. Use of force could well provoke violence apart from deepening hostility and sowing the seeds of permanent discord between the Pashtuns and the Punjabis.[50] For example, till now, the Pashtun tribes took pride in being called the 'unpaid defenders' of Pakistan's frontiers. Would they be any longer?[51]

As the *Dawn* puts it: 'Heavy-handedness towards the movement can only lead to what is most feared—the hardening of their disaffection and the potential for violent factions to emerge'.[52] Prudence would dictate that the army seek a peaceful solution; any miscalculation by the army or the PTM could potentially risk a civil war. Given its resources and firepower, the army would prevail but may have to pay a heavy price.[53]

A similar rights movement in East Pakistan ultimately led to the creation of Bangladesh in 1971. It is quite likely that if the genuine demands of the Pashtuns are not met and they continue to be alienated and subjected to further violence the PTM could well sow the seeds for the further break-up of

Pakistan.⁵⁴ Unlike the Sindhis and the Baloch and like the Bengalis, the Pashtuns have a critical mass of population.

Interestingly, one of the arguments frequently made in Pakistan is that the military regime of Gen Yahya Khan had imposed a near total media censorship about the 1971 crisis that led to the break-up of the country. The argument made is that had an independent media existed, the reality of the situation in East Pakistan could have been made known to the public and the catastrophe of civil war and the break-up of the country perhaps avoided. What is happening today with the Pashtun protests being censored, despite a free press, is a hark-back to the manner how the Bengali protests were handled. Will the results be any different?

Noted journalist Saleem Safi perhaps best summarized the situation: 'The whole country, the Pashtun belt in particular, is once again inching closer towards a new, dangerous and gory crisis. The situation has reached an alarming level and if both sides don't come to their senses, it could result in a national calamity.' He added, "The new unfolding crisis...could lead to serious repercussions that could be more severe than those of the war on terror."⁵⁵

NOTES

1. There are an estimated 37 million Pashtuns in Pakistan constituting nearly 15.42 per cent of the population.
2. Afrasiab Khattak, "A Year Later, a Civil Rights Movement Soldiers on in Pakistan", The Diplomat, Tokyo, February 1, 2019.
3. For a detailed review of the start of the movement, please see the author's article titled: 'Pakistan: Significance of Pashtun Protests' in this volume.
4. Editorial, "A crime unpunished", Dawn, Islamabad, January 6, 2019.
5. Abubakar Siddique, "The Pashtuns' Year Of Living Dangerously", The American Interest, Washington DC, March 8, 2019.
6. Manzoor Ahmad Pashteen, "The Military Says Pashtuns Are Traitors. We Just Want Our Rights", The New York Times, February 11, 2019.
7. Afrasiab Khattak, "A Year Later, a Civil Rights Movement Soldiers on in Pakistan", The Diplomat, Tokyo, February 1, 2019.
8. Ghulam Qadir Khan, "Under the debris", Dawn, Islamabad, October 22, 2018.
9. Manzoor Ahmad Pashteen, "The Military Says Pashtuns Are Traitors. We Just Want Our Rights", The New York Times, February 11, 2019.
10. M Ilyas Khan, "A protest Pakistan wants to hide from the world", BBC, London, February 7, 2019.
11. Zahid Hussain, "Dialogue works better", Dawn, Islamabad, May 1, 2019.
12. Manzoor Ahmad Pashteen, "The Military Says Pashtuns Are Traitors. We Just Want Our Rights", The New York Times, February 11, 2019.

13. S M Hali, "PTM—one year on", Daily Times, Lahore, February 2, 2019.
14. Afrasiab Khattak, "A Year Later, a Civil Rights Movement Soldiers on in Pakistan", The Diplomat, Tokyo, 01 February 2019.
15. "PTM's demands 'justified': Zardari", Dawn, Islamabad, May 1 2019.
16. Amir Wasim, "PTM asked to nominate focal person, present demands", Dawn, Islamabad, April 17, 2019.
17. "State and the PTM", The Express Tribune, Karachi, May 1, 2019.
18. "PM And The PTM", The Nation, Lahore, April 21, 2019.
19. Dilawar Khan Wazir, "Foreign-funded elements behind Fata unrest: Imran", Dawn, Islamabad, April 25, 2019
20. Mohsin Raza Malik, "PTM: The agenda and propaganda", The Nation, Lahore, January 8, 2019.
21. Sadia Qasim Shah, "Bannu varsity bans entry of Manzoor Pashteen", Dawn, Islamabad, May 10, 2018.
22. Mansoor Ali, "Thousands of PTM protesters rally for their rights in North Waziristan", Daily Times, Lahore, April 15 2019.
23. Dr Abdul-Qayum Mohmand, "The Miranshah Jalsa", Daily Times, Lahore, April 18, 2019.
24. Irfan Khan, "PTM's grievance must be addressed", Daily Times, Lahore, February 6, 2019.
25. Hurmat Ali Shah, Pashtuns and the Center–II, The Friday Times, Lahore, January 25, 2019.
26. Dr Farhat Taj, "PTM–an opportunity for rule of law in Pakistan: Part-I", Daily Times, March 21 2019.
27. Abubakar Siddique, "The Pashtuns' Year Of Living Dangerously", The American Interest, Washington DC, March 8, 2019
28. Gul Bukhari, "Year after Pashtun protests, Pakistan military is on arrest spree as civilians fight back", The Print, New Delhi, February 11, 2019.
29. "Detained activists", Dawn, Islamabad, February 9, 2019.
30. Editorial, "The Right To Protest", The Nation, Lahore, February 10, 2019.
31. Trigger-happy officials of the Punjab Police in January 2019 had sprayed a car with bullets near Sahiwal, killing four people including a couple, their teenage daughter and their driver.
32. Baqir Sajjad Syed, "'Hybrid war' imposed on country to internally weaken it," says Bajwa, Dawn, Islamabad, April 15, 2018.
33. "Army will continue to exercise restraint, has no role in conduct of elections," DG ISPR, Dawn, Islamabad, June 4, 2018.
34. Umber Khairi, "Rights and wrongs", The News, Karachi, March 24, 2019.
35. Editorial, "Adopt Conciliation", The Nation, Lahore, January 23, 2019.
36. Muhammad Amir Rana, "US-Taliban talks to decide TTP's fate, PTM's future", Dawn, Islamabad, January 29, 2019.
37. Editorial, "Going for the PTM", Daily Times, Lahore, May 1, 2019.
38. Baqir Sajjad Syed and Syed Irfan Raza, "Foreign spy agencies fund PTM, says army", Dawn, Islamabad, April 30, 2019.
39. Editorial, "DG ISPR's presser", Business Recorder, Karachi, May 1, 2019.

40. Editorial, Who is a traitor?, Dawn, Islamabad, May 1, 2019.
41. Muhammad Amir Rana, "Rights outside faith's domain", Dawn, Islamabad, February 10, 2019.
42. "Afghan president backs Islamabad sit-in", *Dawn*, Islamabad, February 10, 2018.
43. Karim Amini, "Issues Around PTM An Internal Matter Of Pakistan: Rahimi", Tolo News, February 9, 2019.
44. Editorial, "PTM's Trojan Horse", The Nation, Lahore, February 9, 2019.
45. "HRW Calls For 'Transparent Probe' Into PTM Member's Death", Tolo News, Kabul, February 16, 2019.
46. Afrasiab Khattak, "A Year Later, a Civil Rights Movement Soldiers on in Pakistan", The Diplomat, Tokyo, February 01, 2019.
47. Gul Bukhari, "Year after Pashtun protests, Pakistan military is on arrest spree as civilians fight back", ThePrint, New Delhi, February 11, 2019.
48. Farman Kakar, 'The question of Pashtun integration', The News, Karachi, May 1, 2019.
49. Umber Khairi, "Who's the enemy here?", TheNews, Karachi, February 10, 2019.
50. Rustam Shah Mohmand, "PTM and a myopic approach to crisis management", The Express Tribune, Karachi, May 3, 2019.
51. Daud Khan, 'Embrace the Pashtun', The Nation, Lahore, April 6, 2019.
52. Editorial, "Genuine engagement", Dawn, Islamabad, January 24, 2019.
53. Dr Ejaz Hussain, "PTM versus the Military: the way forward", Daily Times, Lahore, May 1, 2019.
54. Taha Siddiqui, "The PTM in Pakistan: Another Bangladesh in the making?", Al Jazeera, Doha, January 13, 2019.
55. Saleem Safi, "On the brink", The News, Karachi, February 10, 2019.

10

Pakistan and FATF[1]

Arvind Gupta

The Financial Action Task Force (FATF), set up in 1989 following a G-7 resolution, provides the international standards for anti-money laundering and combating terrorist financing (AML/CFT). An inter-governmental organisation with 38 members and two observers, the FATF is a policy-making body which sets "standards and promotes effective implementation of legal, regulatory and operational measures for combating money laundering, terrorist financing and other related threats to the integrity of the international financial system."[2]

From time to time the FATF issues 'guidelines' on the subject and carries out the assessment of the AML/CFT regimes in member-countries and provides them guidance for improvement. It has developed detailed methodologies in this regard. The methodology emphasizes the importance of structural elements such as political stability, high-level commitments, the rule of law, independent judicial structure, accountability, integrity, transparency, etc., for efficient and durable AML/CFT measures. At the same time, it takes note of the significance of contextual factors such as the level of corruption and the maturity of the regulatory and supervisory regime in the country as affecting the AML/CFT measures.[3]

The FATF has been monitoring Pakistan for some time now. Pakistan, on whose soil several terrorist groups operate freely and whose agencies are known to have created and supported many of these groups, is an obvious weak point in the international fight against terrorist financing.

Countries with Strategic Deficiencies

The FATF has identified several countries that have 'strategic deficiencies' in their AML/CFT regimes. As on October 2018, these were: The Bahamas, Botswana, Ethiopia, Ghana, Pakistan, Serbia, Sri Lanka, Syria, Trinidad and Tobago, Tunisia and Yemen. The FATF remains engaged with these countries monitoring their progress. It gives them ample time to improve their AML/CFT regimes which is often an incremental process. The cases of Iran and North Korea are instructive to understand how FATF goes about its business. For instance, in 2016, the FATF received high-level political commitments from Iran that it would address AML/CFT deficiencies. As a result, the FATF decided in February 2018 not to press for counter-measures against Iran. However, it also decided that Iran would remain in the so-called 'FATF Public Statement' until it completes its action plan. Thus Iran has been given time but it remains in the FATF list of countries with "strategic deficiencies."[4,5]

What happens if the country concerned does not comply despite repeated persuasions? In such cases, FATF calls upon its member-countries to take 'counter measures.' The case of North Korea is illustrative. According to a public statement by the FATF,

> "... Further, the FATF has serious concerns with the threat posed by the DPRK's illicit activities related to the proliferation of weapons of mass destruction (WMDs) and its financing...the FATF further calls on its members and urges all jurisdictions to apply effective counter-measures, and targeted financial sanctions in accordance with applicable United Nations Security Council Resolutions, to protect their financial sectors from money laundering, financing of terrorism and WMD proliferation financing (ML/FT/PF) risks emanating from the DPRK."[6]

Pakistan and the FATF

Pakistan has been on the FATF's watch list, popularly called the 'grey list', for quite some time now. The FATF found a number of 'strategic deficiencies' in Pakistan's AML/CFT regime. It wanted Pakistan to demonstrate that:

1. Terror Financing (TF) risks are properly identified, assessed, and that supervision is applied on a risk-sensitive basis;
2. Remedial actions and sanctions are applied and complied with by financial institutions in cases of AML/CFT violations;
3. Competent authorities take enforcement action against illegal money or value transfer services (MVTS) in a coordinated fashion;

4. Authorities are identifying cash couriers and enforcing control over the illicit movement of currency and understanding the risk of cash couriers being used for TF;
5. The coordination between provincial and federal authorities on combating TF risks is improved;
6. The law enforcement agencies (LEAs) identify and investigate "the widest range of TF activity"; prosecute targeted persons and identities;
7. Terror financing prosecutions result in effective, proportionate and dissuasive sanctions and enhancing the capacity and support for prosecutors and the judiciary;
8. Comprehensive financial sanctions are imposed against all 1,267 and 1,373 designated terrorists and those acting for or on their behalf, "including preventing the raising and moving of funds, identifying and freezing assets (movable and immovable), and prohibiting access to funds and financial services";
9. Penalties are enforced against federal and provincial authorities who violate TF provisions; and,
10. Designated persons are deprived of their resources and the usage of the resources.

From the above summation, it is clear that Pakistan's record in countering anti-money laundering and terrorist financing is extremely problematic. Despite assurances, Pakistan has not been able to satisfy the FATF. That is why it has been put on the watch list. Whether counter measures against Pakistan would be applied remains to be seen.

A FATF week-long meeting is being held in Paris from 18 February. It comes soon after the Pulwama terrorist attack owned by the Jaish-e-Mohammad (JeM). This terrorist group is linked with the Al-Qaeda and has committed several high-profile attacks in India in recent years including the attack on the Indian Parliament, J&K Assembly, Pathankot air base, Uri army base, Gurdaspur and in Pulwama. The leader of the JeM, Masood Azhar, lives in Bahawalpur, Pakistan and holds rallies all over the country. He should be the first to be booked by Pakistan under the FATF guidelines.

The FATF should be persuaded not to take Pakistan's anti-terror financing violations lightly and initiate counter-measures against it. This will require hard work on the diplomatic front, in particular with the USA and the European Union (EU). China can be expected to bail out Pakistan. In the case of North Korea, the FATF could call for 'counter measures' because there are several existing UN Security Council Resolutions against North Korea because of the latter's nuclear and missiles proliferation activities. This is not the case with Pakistan, so it remains to be seen whether Pakistan will be treated the same way as North Korea or will it again be let off lightly.

NOTES

1. First published by VIF on 18 February 2019, https://www.vifindia.org/2019/february/18/fatf-and-pakistan
2. "Who we are", at http://www.fatf-gafi.org/about/ accessed on 18.2.2019 [Accessed February 18, 2019]
3. http://www.fatgafi.org/media/fatf/documents/methodology/FATF%20Methodology%2022%20Feb%202013.pdf [accessed on February, 2019]
4. Link: http://www.fatf-gafi.org/publications/high-riskandnoncooperativejurisdictions/documents/public-statement-june-2018.html [Accessed on February 18, 2019].
5. Link: http://www.fatf-gafi.org/publications/high-riskandnon-cooperativejurisdictions/documents/public-statement-october-2018.html [Accessed on February 18, 2019].
6. Link: http://www.fatf-gafi.org/countries/a-c/bahamas/documents/fatf-compliance-october-2018.html, [accessed on February 18, 2019].

11

Pakistani Economy: Challenges in 2018-19

Prateek Joshi

Introduction

While the year 2018 was a watershed year for Pakistani politics, challenges to the nation's economy grew manifold. As a report in *Dawn* summarized the prevailing condition, "Pakistan's economy buckled under increasing pressure, with decreasing foreign exchange reserves, increasing trade deficit, circular debt as well as foreign loans taking a toll on macroeconomic health."[1] Besides its poll promise of rooting out corruption, the other factors driving the popularity of the Pakistan Tehreek-e-Insaf (PTI) was its poll promise of employment generation, structural economic reforms and eventually ridding Pakistan of blackmail by international financial institutions. Generation of 10 million new jobs, tax reforms, revival of ailing public sector enterprises and making the China Pakistan Economic Corridor (CPEC) more inclusive and accountable were some of key promises made in the PTI's manifesto, which was titled "The Road to Naya Pakistan."[2]

This article, while discussing the challenges inherited by the new government, stresses on the structural trap facing the Pakistani economy, where mounting debts have a direct bearing on the nation's fiscal/monetary policies. In addition, the government's negotiations with the International Monetary Fund (IMF) and its subsequent economic adjustments based on the latter's directions have worsened the domestic economic situation in the short run. The resulting inflation and the pressure to carry out structural reforms risk eroding the populist support base that brought Prime Minister Imran Khan to power. The resignation of Finance Minister Asad Umar on April 18 points towards the precarious situation the PTI finds itself in.[3] These ongoing adjustments would have a direct short to medium-term impact on the common citizens especially in the form of inflation, rupee depreciation, financial market turbulences as well as interest rate hikes. While these turbulences limit the ruling government's ability to implement speedy reforms, access to an IMF loan would have been impossible without their implementation. The government's pre-requisites to obtain the bailout seem to have worked as the IMF reached a $6 billion staff-level agreement with Pakistan, but these measures come with strong costs attached given the crisis-like situation of the economy.

To understand the making of the present crisis, it becomes imperative to begin by looking into the economic indicators at the end of the last fiscal year (FY), followed by the PTI's action plan to deal with the crisis.

Pre-election Situation

The structural crisis Pakistan's economy has been facing for many years began to show signs of stress as the new dispensation took charge in August 2018. This is easily explained by the unsustainable debt indicators during the last days of the Pakistan Muslim League-Nawaz (PML-N) led government:[4]

1. Domestic debt and liabilities rose from 9.76 trillion rupees to 17 trillion rupees between 2013 and 2018, that is, the period corresponding with the PML-N's tenure.
2. Budget Deficit rose from 1.8 trillion rupees in FY 2016-17 to 2.2 trillion rupees in FY 2017-18, amounting to 6.6 per cent of the Gross Domestic Product (GDP).
3. External debt peaked at $91.8 billion by the end of March 2018, growing at a staggering 9.3 per cent per annum in the last five years.
4. For the FY ending June 30, 2018, the Current Account Deficit (CAD) stood at its highest, amounting to $18 billion (5.7 per cent of the GDP), almost 45 per cent higher than the FY 2017 figure ($12 billion).
5. Foreign exchange (forex) reserves dropped to $9 billion, an amount enough to finance only six weeks of imports. Of this, $6.7 billion were in the form of short-term borrowings.

To make things worse, the PML-N presented a populist budget in April 2018, in which it slashed income tax rates for those in the highest income bracket, along with announcing other sops at the cost of raising revenues.[5] Despite the existing pressures, the defence budget was hiked by 20 per cent (compared to the previous year's budget) to approximately $9.6 billion.[6] Prime Minister Shahid Khaqan Abbasi announced a generous tax amnesty scheme with massive hopes of recovering money stashed overseas but it failed to gain traction.[7] These announcements were made at a time when the Budget Deficit increased to 6.6 per cent (2.2 trillion rupees) of the GDP in FY 2017-18, and was projected to further rise to 7.2 per cent (2.9 trillion rupees) by FY 2018-19.[8] Supplementing the rising domestic debt, the CAD stood at $18.1 billion (5.7 per cent of the GDP) by the end of FY 2017-18.[9] Given these unstable indicators, the PTI embarked on a series of measures simultaneously aiming to rectify the impending crises on the domestic as well as the external front. However, there were no concrete signs of improvement in the indicators for the time being. The PTI, which spearheaded the opposition's voice during the PML-N's tenure has responded to these challenges in more or less the same manner as its predecessor did, thereby negating all the claims it had made when in the opposition. In the past, senior PTI leaders, including Imran Khan and Asad Umar, went on record criticizing the former regimes' dependence on the IMF bailouts that came at the cost of surrendering the nation's sovereignty to foreign institutions.

PTI's Austerity Drive

Broadly, the new government embarked on the twin policy of fiscal profligacy and external borrowings to shore up the falling forex reserves. Citing the PML-N's last budget as "unrealistic," the PTI introduced a supplementary budget in September 2018 which was aimed towards cutting expenditures and raising revenues. Development Expenditure was trimmed by 250 billion rupees to 725 billion rupees.[10] Tax cuts announced by the outgoing PML-N government for those in the top income bracket were rolled back.[11] Excise duties on luxury vehicles and Customs duties on 5,000 luxury items were raised. The target was to raise $1.5 billion additional revenue and capping the Budget deficit at around 5 per cent of the GDP.[12]

Some other austerity measures were also announced to convince the IMF of the government's attempts to pursue fiscal consolidation. Measures were adopted to cut administrative costs, which included cutting down on some benefits of high-ranking officials and politicians, auction of the car fleet owned by the Prime Minister's Office and retrenchment of staff at the PM House. The data however reveals the futility of this exercise as it was directed to cut the annual 221 billion rupee administrative budget, which is only a miniscule amount of the budget deficit, which is projected to be close to 3 trillion rupees for FY 2018-19.[13]

The PTI came to terms with the prevailing economic situation and shed its long-standing criticism on international lending institutions. In October, the Finance Minister announced the decision to go to the IMF to negotiate for the 13th bailout.[14] The above-mentioned measures were taken to signal the IMF about Pakistan's readiness to carry out reforms. Nevertheless, the government went for the IMF option only after its borrowings did not bring the desired inflows. The most important question is how long can the government continue to borrow when there is no policy measure to boost its forex reserves?

Forex Borrowings: Gauging Sustainability

Only a few weeks after the formation of the new government, forex reserves hit a four-year low when they plummeted to $8.4 billion, an amount able to sustain six weeks of imports. By January 2019, the reserves were further down to $6.6 billion.[15] Immediately after assuming the Prime Ministership, Imran Khan embarked on multiple foreign visits with the sole purpose of obtaining short-term borrowings to shore up the falling forex reserves. The visits to the United Arab Emirates (UAE) and Saudi Arabia were successful as Pakistan secured $6.2 billion and $6 billion dollars, respectively, from both the nations, with half of the pledged amount in the nature of currency inflows and the other half in the form of deferred payments on oil purchases. Of the $3 billion pledged by the UAE, $2 billion was obtained but Pakistan did not receive the $3.2 billion in deferred payments for oil purchases from the UAE.

From the beginning of FY 2018 to the end of March 2019, Pakistan received a total of $9.1 billion to shore up its forex reserves ($4.1 billion from China, $3 billion from Saudi Arabia and $2 billion from the UAE). These inflows are however not grants but are in the form of short-term loans that have to be paid back, with 3.2 per cent and 3 per cent rate of interest charged by the UAE and Saudi Arabia, respectively. In addition, the government also launched $1 billion worth of Dollar-denominated Diaspora Bonds in January to tap overseas Pakistanis as well as Pakistanis with offshore accounts at an attractive rate of "6.25% interest rate for three years and in five-year bonds at 6.75% return."[16]

Despite these injections, forex reserves have hovered around $8 billion with the larger challenge being the financing gap at the end of FY 2018-19, which was estimated by the outgoing Finance Minister Asad Umar to be around $12 billion, followed by $7-8 billion gap expected by FY 2019-20.[17]

Rupee Depreciation and Mounting Current Account Deficit (CAD)

From FY 2014-15 onwards, the CAD registered an exponential increase due to rising imports and stagnating exports. From $3.2 billion in 2014-15, the CAD rose to $5.45 billion in 2015-16, $12.94 billion in 2016-17 (4.1% of GDP) and further to $18 billion (5.8% of GDP) in FY 2017-18; the increase being a staggering 44 per cent in FY 2017-18.[18]

Year 2018 and the first few months of 2019 have not augured well for the Pakistani rupee, which has been on the downswing since December 2017, when the State Bank of Pakistan (SBP) embarked on a devaluation spree to boost exports and discourage imports. Between December 2017 and December 2018, the SBP devalued the rupee by approximately 35 per cent, as there have been no other potent alternative to stall the burgeoning CAD.[19] The CAD had been on the rise from 2016 onwards and the devaluation policy came into effect from 2018 onwards only. In other words, the rupee had been kept deliberately overvalued over the three-year phase (2014-17) and its stability could be maintained only by pumping out extra dollars from the forex reserves.[20] In particular, it was under former Finance Minister Ishaq Dar that the government adopted the managed-float regime and kept the rupee under strict check by losing out by selling foreign exchange in the process. During Dar's tenure as the Finance Minister until his ouster in July 2017, the rupee depreciated marginally from 98 to 105 per dollar.[21] The pressure was not felt since the forex loss was compensated by inflows from the 12th IMF bailout, "bilateral loans from friendly countries, bond auctions in foreign markets and the privatisation of state-owned enterprises."[22]

The free fall began a few months after Dar's departure and continued as the new dispensation took charge of the government.[23] This is because the old policy of discarding forex to keep the rupee stable had become unsustainable and as a result, the rupee was allowed to depreciate from December 2017 onwards.

The IMF Route

The decision to go to the IMF has been amongst the most notable "U-turns" taken by the Imran Khan government, given the PTI's historic opposition to international lending institutions. The government decided to go ahead with the negotiations even as the $6.6 billion amount borrowed as part of the 12th bailout is yet to be repaid.[24] Calculating from Pakistan's Special Drawing Rights (SDR) Quota (Pakistan holds 2,031 million SDRs), it is estimated that Pakistan was eligible to borrow around $6 billion under the standard borrowing route, which falls under Extended Funding Facility's Normal Access conditions. This also corresponds to the $6 billion bailout amount the IMF agreed to lend to Pakistan.

The successive rounds of talks between IMF officials and Islamabad show that structural reforms remain a sticking point between both the sides due to Islamabad's reluctance to carry them out according to IMF's expected terms. The IMF's larger concern is that if Islamabad fails to implement the prescribed structural reforms, the next bailout would be wasted either in settling external deficits or financing the CPEC loans.

However, within 100 days of taking charge, the government did begin working in line with the IMF's directions by increasing taxes in the supplementary budget as mentioned above, raised the prices of fuel and other utilities but the IMF insisted on more reforms, which stood in contrast with the PTI's populist economic agenda.[25]

The IMF has long insisted on free float of the rupee, since it still considers it as over-valued, despite multiple rounds of devaluation. On the fiscal front, raising electricity and fuel tariffs and General Sales Taxes (GST) have been strongly recommended towards achieving a medium-term fiscal consolidation.[26] Other recommendations include working towards minimizing the losses of public sector enterprises, privatization and reforming the energy sector (whose circular debt stood at 1.4 trillion rupees by January 2019). In the February 10, 2019 meeting between the IMF chief and Prime Minister Imran Khan in Dubai, the IMF expressed its willingness to support the Pakistan government, provided the above-stated reforms were implemented. Following the IMF directions, the government has been raising the prices of basic utilities and by the end of March 2019, along with rising food prices, fuel prices were once again increased by 6.5 per cent.

As per the Pakistan Bureau of Statistics (PBS), inflation stood at 9.4 per cent in March 2019, the highest in the last five years and even overshot the government's projection of 6 per cent for FY 2018-19.[27] In comparison, the average inflation stood at 3.9 per cent in FY 2017-18 and 4.16 per cent in the year before.[28] Also, as directed by the IMF, the SBP raised interest rates to

10.75 per cent by March to squeeze excess liquidity from the economy.[29] There has been a 6.5 per cent increase in interest rates since January 2018.[30]

In the latest round of talks held in April 2019 in Washington, an in-principle agreement was reportedly reached on a bailout program. Irrespective of the IMF's push, the Pakistani economy needs to implement structural reforms to get rid of these unsustainable debt cycles and increase its revenue generation capacity in the medium run.

The Road Ahead

After securing 5 per cent plus growth rate in FY 2017-18, efforts towards fiscal consolidation, monetary squeeze and the resultant high inflation have lowered the growth projections for FY 2018-19. With initial forecasts projecting more than 6 per cent growth rate, pressures on the economy have reduced the projections to below 4 per cent.[31] The SBP's latest forecast in April 2019 lowered the growth projection from an earlier estimate of 6.2 per cent to 4 per cent.[32] The fiscal deficit is projected to hover around 6-7 per cent of the GDP.

The Asian Development Bank (ADB) estimated the nation's growth rate to fall to 3.9 per cent.[33] Similar projections were also released by Fitch (an international credit rating agency), which pegged the growth rate at 4.4 per cent due to the policy of tightening fiscal and monetary conditions.[34] Further, the World Bank also lowered its estimates to 3.4 per cent and 2.7 per cent for FY 2019-20. The unanimity is further strengthened with estimates released by the IMF. The IMF, in its annual report titled World Economic Outlook, stated that Pakistan's growth rate would further reduce to 2.5 per cent and the trend would continue until 2024 if it did not implement structural reforms.[35] Citing the dangers from external deficit, the report estimates the CAD at 5.2 per cent of the GDP for FY 2018-19, which is even higher than the Finance Ministry's estimate.

In short, fiscal and monetary tightening, in the absence of any strong measures to boost the government's earnings (via taxation or export-led growth) solely contributed to these sluggish projections.

The only positive factor is the stable inflow of remittances mostly from Gulf and Arab nations to the tune of approximately $19.6 billion in FY 2017-18 which is expected to rise to $22 billion by the end of FY 2018-19.[36] However, remittances are dependent on the economic stability of those economies. Pakistan would need to focus on boosting its forex earnings. Besides the challenge from growing imports, the CPEC and the 12th IMF bailout loan related repayments would begin soon.

On the domestic front, the government has been unable to allay the rising public anger. In the absence of any immediate relief to slowing growth projections and high inflation, the government has resorted to rhetoric and speculation-mongering. Recently, the government claimed to have discovered massive energy reserves in Pakistan and claimed it would allay the nation's economic woes. The abrupt resignation of the Finance Minister and Imran's new choice of Abdul Hafiz Shaikh (former finance minister in the PPP government) as his new Financial Advisor only added another old hand to Imran's "new team."

On May 12, 2019, Pakistan and the IMF reached an agreement over a $6 billion bailout to be disbursed over a period of three years. As per Financial Advisor Sheikh, the agreement would enable the government to further borrow $2-3 billion from the World Bank and the ADB. All these efforts notwithstanding, given the state of the economy, the amount not only falls short to revive the severely debt-ridden economy, but also makes up for the shortfall in the balance of payments. The only viable solutions happen to be structural adjustments, tax reforms and fiscal adjustments, which may be beneficial in the long run but for now have made the government unpopular.

NOTES

1. Asad Farooq, "These 19 developments shaped Pakistan's economic future in 2018", *Dawn*, Islamabad, December 27, 2018.
2. Fahad Chaudhary, "Imran Khan unveils PTI manifesto 'Road to Naya Pakistan'", *Dawn*, Islamabad, July 9, 2018.
3. "Pakistan's Finance Minister Asad Umar quits ahead of IMF deal", *Economic Times*, Mumbai, April 19, 2019.
4. Prateek Joshi, "Pakistan Economy: Challenges Ahead for the new Government", Vivekananda International Foundation, August 30, 2018.
5. "Budget 2018-19: Standout features and key talking points", *Dawn*, Islamabad, April 28, 2018.
6. Ibid.
7. "PM announces simplified income tax package, amnesty scheme for foreign assets", *Dawn*, Islamabad, April 5, 2018.
8. Shahbaz Rana, "Pakistan's debt pile to swell to 84.1% of GDP by 2023", *Express Tribune*, Karachi, April 11, 2019.
9. Erum Zaidi, "Deficit rises to $18 billion: Current account deficit widens to 5.7 % of GDP in FY2018", *The News International*, Karachi, April 11, 2019.

10. Sanaullah Khan, "Government cuts development spending, increases taxes on country's elite", *Dawn*, Islamabad, September 18, 2018.
11. Ibid.
12. Ibid.
13. Khalid Qayum, Kamran Haider and Ismail Dilawar, "Buffaloes, BMWs and Free Lunches End in Pakistan Austerity Drive", Bloomberg, New York, September 19, 2018.
14. "Cash-strapped Pakistan to approach IMF for bailout package", *Economic Times*, Mumbai, October 9, 2018.
15. "China pumps-in USD 2.2 billion in Pakistan's dwindling forex reserves", *Economic Times*, Mumbai, January 25, 2019.
16. Shahbaz Rana, "Pakistanis having offshore accounts can invest in diaspora bonds", *Express Tribune*, Karachi, February 9, 2019.
17. "China pumps-in USD 2.2 billion in Pakistan's dwindling forex reserves", *Economic Times*, Mumbai, January 25, 2019.
18. Salman Siddiqui, "Pakistan's current account deficit peaks at $17.99b", *Express Tribune*, Karachi, July 20, 2018.
19. "Pakistani rupee plunges about 6% in what traders say could be a central bank devaluation", CNBC, New Jersey, October 9, 2018.
20. Hussain Zaidi, "Was the rupee depreciation avoidable?", *Dawn*, Islamabad, July 2, 2018.
21. Khurran Hussain, "Falling Rupee", *Dawn*, Islamabad, July 14, 2018.
22. Kazim Alam, "The aftershocks of a fallen rupee", *Dawn*, Islamabad, March 26, 2019.
23. Ibid.
24. First Post Program Monitoring Discussion, Press Release, Staff Report, Statement by Staff and Statement by Executive Director for Pakistan, IMF, March 5, 2018.
25. News Desk, "Fiscal, monetary policies in line with required economic reforms: Asad Umar", *The Express Tribune*, Karachi, December 12, 2018.
26. Anwar Iqbal, "IMF calls for further hike in gas, power tariffs", *Dawn*, Islamabad, October 5, 2018.
27. Mubarak Zeb Khan, "Inflation hits 9.4 pc, highest in five years", *Dawn*, Islamabad, April 2, 2019.
28. Ibid.
29. Ibid.
30. "Pakistan raises key interest rate to 12.25 per cent", *New Indian Express*, Chennai, May 20, 2019.
31. Salman Siddiqui, "SBP expects slowdown in economic growth to 4-4.5%", *The Express Tribune*, Karachi, January 30, 2019.
32. Ibid.
33. "Pakistan's GDP to decelerate to 3.9% in 2019: Asian Development Bank", *Business Today*, New Delhi, April 3, 2019.
34. Jamie Mackenzie, "Pakistan central bank sees 2019 GDP growth slowing to 3.5-4.0 %", Reuters, London, March 25, 2019.
35. Shahbaz Rana, "IMF puts country's growth rate at 2.5%", *The Express Tribune*, Karachi, April 10, 2019.
36. Muzaffar Rizvi, "Pakistan remittances may hit $22 billion in 2018-19", *Khaleej Times*, Dubai, October 30, 2018.

12

Emerging Situation in Pakistan in 2019[1]

Dr. Shalini Chawla

Pakistan presently faces some critical challenges but also has few opportunities it can build on. The challenges include Pakistan's severe economic crisis, Imran's proclaimed fight against corruption and corrupt politicians, water crisis, extremism in society, tough stance of the Trump Administration and mounting pressure from the Financial Action Task Force (FATF). However, the opportunities offered by the China-Pakistan Economic Corridor (CPEC), a newly-elected "clean" Prime Minister who promised "Naya Pakistan" and consistent support from China, Saudi Arabia and the UAE are considerable. 2018 witnessed many predictable and at the same time unconventional developments for Pakistan. It would be useful to analyse these developments to be able to have an insight into where Pakistan is heading in 2019.

Civil-Military Relations have perpetually been a matter of great debate in Pakistan with the military dominating the core strategic decision-making. During the 2018 elections, the military and Imran Khan complemented each other's 'vital requirements'. The cricketer wanted to be in power and the military found a seemly candidate in Imran who was fully in sync with their objectives and actions and willing to operate within the 'defined boundaries' of the civilian leadership. The elections witnessed every possible military and ISI-sponsored dirty tactic to support the PTI's mammoth victory. The judiciary, the National Accountability Bureau and the military collaborated 'rather well' for the selection of the desired Prime Minister. Nawaz Sharif, his family and most of the loyal PML-N aides have been snared in legal battles on corruption charges. Although the legitimacy of the PTI-led coalition remains questionable, Imran will stay in power till he oversteps the red lines and does not provoke the deep state. It looks unlikely that he will go against the military any time soon.

The top priority for Imran, undeniably, is managing the looming economic crisis. The current account deficit increased from $2.7 billion in 2015 to $18.2 billion in 2018 (*The Dawn*, 2018). Reports suggest there has been some improvement due to an increase in remittances and deceleration in imports. Pakistan's external debts and liabilities stand at $96.7 billion. Reportedly, debt servicing and defence consume more than 50 per cent of the total budget. Pakistan needs a substantial infusion of economic assistance to avoid a financial breakdown and is looking at various options to relieve its economic woes. The most desirable option is the International Monetary Fund (IMF) bailout.

The IMF has, in the past, given 12 bailouts to Pakistan. The economy requires an urgent IMF bailout of at least $6 billion to stabilise. The IMF has been tough and has been insistent on greater transparency on the CPEC financial transactions. US Secretary of State Mike Pompeo made a strong statement that the IMF bailout cannot be used by Pakistan to repay 'Chinese debt'. CPEC, which is seen by most Pakistanis as a game changer, has apparently added to the debt burden of Pakistan. Chinese debt amounts to approximately 10 per cent of the total debt of Pakistan. The IMF bailout is expected to come with strict conditions and austerity measures such as a tax hike, spending cuts, requirement of greater transparency in financial dealings (including CPEC), demand of structural reforms, etc. CPEC will bring enhanced economic activities but the economic crisis would impact the repayment capability of Pakistan which can adversely affect the Chinese investments.

Pakistan is currently on the grey list of the FATF. Insufficient efforts to curb terror financing and money laundering could lead Pakistan to the FATF 'black list' adding to Pakistan's economic woes. Currently, two countries which are on the FATF black list are Iran and North Korea. The FATF black list would have severe financial implications for Pakistan including increased scrutiny, increased transaction cost, longer transaction time and costly loans. The Asia Pacific Group of FATF visited Pakistan in the second half of 2018 and raised serious concerns including the funding of UN-designated organisations and terrorists. Pakistan is under immense pressure to take convincing steps to evade the FATF black list.

Religious and extremist factions have gained a strong footing in the country. General elections in July 2018 witnessed an alarming development of Hafiz Saeed's party, the Allah-o-Akbar Tehreek (AAT), contesting the elections with over 200 candidates. The Tehreek-e-Labbaik Pakistan (TLP), which basically caught attention after the execution of Mumtaz Qadri, the convicted killer of Punjab Governor Salman Taseer, managed to swing a large number of votes in Karachi and Punjab. Imran's Government encountered a challenge and setback when the TLP threatened protests against the appointment of the Princeton economist, Atif Mian, in the Economic Advisory Council, formed to deal with the looming economic crisis. Imran surrendered to the TLP demands and excluded Atif Mian from the council on account of the fact that he belongs to the Ahmadiyya sect. The incident does project Imran's vulnerability in dealing with extremist and religious factions in future.

The military has gained much more power and has restated its political, strategic and military valour. Core strategic decision-making including the nuclear programme and doctrine, defence budget and procurement, foreign policy vis-à-vis India and Afghanistan remain strictly with the military. Conventional military build-up has been maintained, with focused acquisitions of the Pakistan Air Force and maritime strike capabilities of the navy. On the nuclear front, the military seems to be extremely confident of pronounced "full spectrum deterrence." Pakistan's reliance on nuclear weapons and assertion of 'first use' is likely to increase due to mounting insecurities within.

On the external front, Pakistan's relationship with the USA has been under stress and the Trump Administration has adopted a strict posturing towards Pakistan, drastically reducing financial and security assistance. Pakistan, in its efforts to appease the USA, did manage to facilitate the Afghan Taliban meeting with the USA. Islamabad realises the criticality of its relationship with the USA given Washington's decisive role in the leading international financial institutions.

The China-Pakistan relationship remains an all-weather friendship and Pakistanis are extremely confident of the support they will continue to receive from Beijing. Despite some apprehensions which arose after the attack on the Chinese consulate by Baloch separatists, the China-Pakistan relationship is expected to sustain and maintain the momentum.

The India-Pakistan relationship has hit an extremely low point over the last couple of years and New Delhi has maintained its position on 'conditional dialogue' with Pakistan. The opening of the Kartarpur Corridor might have raised hopes for some sections, but the fact remains that Pakistan needs to demonstrate a serious resolve to alter its policy of supporting terrorism against

India. With the civilian leadership in Pakistan being completely under the shadow of the military, the resolve is unlikely to happen any time soon.

Some trends that can be forecast for 2019 are as follows:

- Imran Khan will not rock the boat at the domestic level. He will try to remain within the boundaries defined by the military on critical strategic issues.
- Civil-military relations will remain cautiously comfortable in 2019.
- Imran's Government is likely to continue placating religious and extremist parties.
- The IMF bailout is expected to come for Pakistan as a reliever but the country will have to deal with the conditions.
- Looking into the history of Pakistan's crisis management, it looks like it will manage to stay away from the FATF black list. Also, China, Vice President of FATF, is expected to play a favourable role for Pakistan in the FATF decision-making this year.
- Military build-up will continue primarily with Chinese assistance. Expansion of the nuclear arsenal will continue and Islamabad's reliance on nuclear weapons is likely to increase.
- Pakistan's relationship with China will continue to grow and maintain the momentum of cooperation.
- Relationship with the USA will continue to be difficult. Pakistan is expected to continue efforts to pacify the Trump Administration.
- Pakistan has a military dominated civilian authority and given that India is getting ready for elections in 2019, its relationship with India will continue to face its challenges and there appears no possibility of any breakthrough in the near future.

NOTES

1   First published by VIF 09 January 2019, https://www.vifindia.org/2019/january/09/emerging-situation-in-pakistan-in-2019

EXTERNAL

13

Pakistan under Imran Khan: What's in it for Indo-Pak Relations[1]

Lt. General S. A. Hasnain

Whoever heard Pakistan's Prime Minister (Designate) Imran Khan speak on 26 July 2018 after it became quite evident that the election had gone his way would have had to change his image in the mind's eye to make any sense of it at all. We have seen him in India over the years in friendlier times. The flamboyant playboy image, his strong competitiveness and hugely India-friendly leaning signified his personality. Those were the days when people wondered why the attitude of Imran Khan could not be replicated by the establishment in Pakistan which was always unfriendly. It is now becoming quite clear to all that in order to be high in the pecking order in Pakistan you just have to simply change your colours much like the chameleon. In Imran's case, that change over became a makeover; his entire personality has undergone a change as against the other mainstream faces such as Nawaz Sharif and Bilawal Bhutto.

The Pakistan Army, which exercises control over the destiny of Pakistan in many ways, realised that its sojourn with the first two mainstream political parties—the Pakistan People's Party (PPP) and the Pakistan Muslim League–Nawaz (PML-N)—was over. The reason for this was the apparent emboldening of their leaders with the passage of time and attempts to seek an independent line, mostly on the relationship with India. For the Pakistan Army, Imran Khan's Pakistan Tehreek-e-Insaf (PTI) Party, young in comparison and freshly in power in Khyber Pakhtunkhwa (KPK), appeared to have all the boxes ticked as far as national power potential was concerned. Any party so sponsored would obviously be beholden to the sponsor. For the last three years or more the build-up of PTI had been underway.

For Imran Khan's personal survival, a makeover to an Islamist image was necessary in addition to the nationalist image already in existence due him being the captain of Pakistan's Cricket World Cup winning team. In the recent past he has often been referred to as Taliban Khan and Jihadi Khan after he helped paralyse the city of Islamabad a few times to protest corruption in the then existing PML-N government. Whether the Pakistan Army actively connived with the Pakistan Election Commission to have the PTI come to power may eventually become inconsequential because a very appropriately orchestrated result has come to be. The PTI is there and yet not; it will need the support of some parties to make a government. The stability would have been much higher if the PTI had scored a full victory but that may have emboldened it a little too early. In other words, the control of the deep state over Imran Khan is complete.

Given the above situation, does anyone in India perceive better times ahead as far as Indo-Pakistan relations are concerned? Slivers of hope have arisen in the recent past. The arrival of General Qamar Bajwa as Pakistan's Army Chief a year and a half ago sent some positive signals. He was known to be well educated and someone who could understand the larger interests of Pakistan in peace with India in order to resolve Pakistan's far more serious social and economic problems. However, that perception did not translate into anything substantial despite a much-hyped Bajwa Doctrine. The build-up to the Pakistan election of 2018 was arranged by the Pakistan Army's near-total connivance with the higher judiciary and a subjugated media to prevent the PML-N returning to power, because the latter was straining at the leash to be allowed a free hand in the conduct of its India policy. With Imran, therefore, nothing is likely to change. Mindsets and history do not allow changes to occur; only circumstances do. So its circumstances that either has to be created or has to come about through trends and events that will change the way in relations are conducted. What could, if at all, these changes possibly be?

One is a possible outreach by India as a fresh initiative. With nine months to another hotly contested general elections in 2019, this is highly unlikely. The National Democratic Alliance (NDA) Government had earlier made an honest attempt, and in fact took the proverbial two steps that Imran Khan spoke of in his recent speech, without receiving even one step in response. Any softening of approach towards Pakistan as an Indian initiative is therefore highly unlikely.

Two, can Imran Khan take the initiative? Given the fact that he is shackled under Army control, makes that least likely. Assuming that he does, the approach that he displayed in his initial speech, of addressing Kashmir as the core issue and accusing the Indian Army of serious human rights violations, is unlikely to create even an iota of the positive environment which would be necessary for India to walk the extra mile, even in a longer time frame.

Three, could there be a set of circumstances dictating Pakistan's internal situation which could trigger a forced policy change and eventually lead to the creation of a better environment. This refers to the Financial Assistance Task Force (FATF)-related strictures against Pakistan asking it to set right its internal mechanisms to prevent financial support to terror networks. With Pakistan's economy in a mess and two billion dollar relief packages already given by China, Pakistan will at some stage need to display more transparency in the measures that it has to undertake to prevent sponsoring of terror. That calls for a proactive Indian approach to ensure that it does. It will need diplomatic initiatives and influencing of the right quarters to ensure that Pakistan's counter-measures include the India-centric jihadi elements that it treats as its strategic assets. The election has produced one positive situation—the relative political marginalisation of the India-focused jihadi groups. Hafiz Sayeed and his Milli Muslim League, riding atop the Allah-o-Akbar Tehreek Party, scored no victories. Can this be exploited or, more importantly, will the Pakistan deep state allow the placement of these assets in cold storage, at least temporarily. Relative control over these elements could create an environment free of jihadi-oriented violence and any major attempts to target India.

The fourth element among these circumstances is the role of China. For many years, Pakistan's emboldened stance of taking on India through the hybrid conflict route has been possible because of the backing from China. It then suited China too. However, 2017-18 have been eventful years in Sino-Indian relations, with its peaks and troughs. The reset in place after Wuhan, Sochi and Qingdao is yet underway and China may well view an improved Indo-Pakistan relationship as beneficial to its larger international interests. Under those circumstances, China's initiative could go far in setting the environment for an improved Indo-Pakistan relationship.

The bottom line Indian requirement that will see any breakthrough is a set of measures by Imran Khan's Pakistan that will place controls over the anti-India jihadi groups in Pakistan. It has to be a verifiable set of measures with meaningful statements in the diplomatic environment. A quiet Line of

Control over an elongated period of time will assist in pegging any process which comprises all this.

Interestingly, a question being asked is whether Prime Minister Narendra Modi should accept Prime Minister (Designate) Imran Khan's possible invitation to attend his swearing-in in the near future. There are no easy answers to this and the Indian Government will have to seriously consider the issue. Possibly, with nine months to the general elections in India and no Pakistani assurance of any follow-up diplomatic initiatives which, any way, will be in the hands of the Pakistan Army, Mr. Modi would stand to lose face. He had tried one transformational moment on 25 Dec 2015 which came a cropper; a second one for no foreseeable gains will not fetch him or India any dividends. Perhaps India's Minister of External Affairs, Mrs. Sushma Swaraj, could be an ideal personality to attend the ceremony.

NOTES

1   First published by VIF on 28 July 2018, https://www.vifindia.org/2018/july/28/pakistan-under-imran-khan-what-s-in-it-for-indo-pakrelations

14

Efficacy of Track II Process in Indo-Pak Relations

C.D. Sahay

ABSTRACT

In modern diplomacy, alternate modes of diplomatic engagements through Back Channel, Track-1.5 and Track-II have come to play an important role and legitimacy in facilitating better understanding between governments. This is valid even amongst countries having a robust state-to-state relation.

In the context of India-Pakistan relations, where the normal channels of engagement through diplomatic representatives and even political leadership have been traditionally weak, quite often even non-existent, the alternate forms of deniable and off-the-record conversations outside public glare can play a critical role.

While Track-IIs under various brand names like Pugwash and Neemrana have been in existence for quite some time, in recent times there has been considerable proliferation with different sets of sponsors, participants and issue-specific agendas. These have had varying degrees of success.

However, given the complexities of problems between the two countries and fairly intense level of mutual suspicion, one gets a sense that compared to Track-II approach, the two countries need to work more through the Track-1.5 and Back Channel modes. Ideally, after the ongoing election process, a combination of the two could be the best option to break the current logjam.

Background

The term Track-II Diplomacy was reportedly coined in 1981 by Joseph V. Montville, a U.S. State Department employee, who argued that while Track

One diplomacy was what diplomats did—formal negotiations between nations—Track-II diplomacy referred to conflict resolution efforts by professional non-governmental conflict resolution practitioners and theorists. "Track Two has as its objective of reduction or resolution of conflict, within a country or between countries, by lowering the anger or tension or fear that exists, through improved communication and a better understanding of each other's point of view."[1]

Montville (Davidson & Montville, 1981) further maintains that there are two basic processes in Track II diplomacy.[2] The first consists of facilitated workshops that bring members of conflicting groups together to develop personal relationships, understand the conflict from the perspective of others, and develop joint strategies for solving the conflict. The second process involves working to shift public opinion: "Here the task is a psychological one which consists of reducing the sense of victimhood of the parties and re-humanizing the image of the adversary."[3]

In the specific context of Track-II diplomacy involving India and Pakistan, in an article for the Ministry of External Affairs on Public Diplomacy in December 2010,[4] former High Commissioner to Pakistan, Amb. G. Parthasarthy reinforced the above view that Track-II exchanges have an invaluable role to play when traditional instruments of negotiation, mediation and conflict management become ineffective and need to be supplemented.

History of India-Pakistan Track-II

Tracing the history of Track-II meetings between India and Pakistan, Amb. Parthasarthy explained that the first attempt at a Track-II approach to problems in Jammu and Kashmir was undertaken by the US-based Kashmir Study Group, headed by, Farookh Kathwari. Prominent American and Pakistani diplomats were associated with this effort with India represented by former Foreign Secretary S.K. Singh and former Vice Chief of Naval Staff, Vice Admiral K.K. Nayyar.

Since then, there have been many initiatives at Track-II engagements between the two countries such as the 'Pugwash Conference', 'Chao Phrya Dialogue', the Ottawa Dialogue and of course the Neemrana initiative, the last being more in the nature of a Track-1.5 engagement suggesting a limited degree of official backing. This is not an exhaustive list since many such initiatives at Track-II engagements are being undertaken by different think-tanks and study centres to bring together strategic experts from the two countries with the objective of creating better understanding, reducing tension and seeking to explore areas of cooperation. Some of the institutes and think-tanks with better resources have even started organising issue-based interactions.

Most of these meetings are held in third countries, basically to avoid public attention. 'Neemrana' has been an exception. The list of participants is determined on the basis of subjects under review. At the end of the discussions, a set of agreed recommendations are drawn up and shared with the decision-makers for whatever its worth.

Some Important Achievements

In this context, one is again tempted to quote from Amb. Parthasarthy's article referred to in para 3 above, wherein he specifically listed out the following important points/achievements of the Pugwash conference in December 2004:

1. Participants acknowledged that the human dimension of the conflict should take priority over geo-strategic considerations;
2. There was need for developing a people-centred approach and making the human dimension of the Kashmir problem part and parcel of the political dialogue at all levels;
3. A prolonged period of non-violence, coupled with genuine social and economic reforms was needed to deflate a great number of problems and help establish a durable and sustainable peace;
4. One cannot expect a society to shift instantly from profound trauma to peace, the report emphasized;
5. There seemed to be much agreement that the UN Resolutions proposing a plebiscite to express the political choices of Kashmiris, of acceding to either India or Pakistan, was now obsolete;
6. There was need for intra-Kashmiri dialogue and process of reconciliation within both sides of Jammu and Kashmir and across the Line of Control; and between people of Jammu and Kashmir and both capitals;
7. Bilateral process should arrive at Kashmiri-specific CBMs. A general consensus developed at the meeting that all forms of violence should end, irrespective of their form or origin;
8. Civil society throughout the state should de-legitimize violence through massive demonstrations;
9. Ceasefire between Pakistan and India on the LoC was already paying dividends, and should be extended within J&K;

10. Training camps and recruitment networks should be dismantled. All parties and individuals should refrain from statements and actions that incite or promote hatred and violence.

To say the least, these recommendations were path-breaking and most of these points of 'agreement' were covered in the then on-going Vajpayee-Musharraf dialogue. This was truly remarkable.

In a similar vein, in one of the later Track-II interactions, the participants, who largely came from Intelligence/security backgrounds, strongly urged the two governments to set up 'Back Channel'[5] contacts between their Intelligence establishments just as the DGMOs had a well-oiled mechanism for dealing with cross-border problems. While one does not know the fate of that recommendation, a recent media report on the post-Pulwama developments did notably refer to contact between the Intelligence officials to convey messages and defuse/manage tension.

Track II: A Mixed Experience due to Inherent Limitations

However, one must hasten to add that not all Track-II initiatives could possibly claim similar achievements. My own experience based on a rather limited exposure to different Track-II processes, is one of mixed satisfaction. The mixed feeling arises out of the inherent limitations of such efforts. For one, the discussants comprise retired officers who bring to the table a great deal of experience but have limited access to the current state of relations beyond what is generally available through media reports and minimal interaction with the current set of decision makers. The participants do not carry a formal brief. Besides, the recommendations end up largely reiterating the stated positions of their respective governments.

That is not to say that these interactions are a waste of time and effort. On the contrary, it must be acknowledged that the wealth of knowledge and experience that the participants bring to the table does help in discussing issues and events in a frank atmosphere, free of any official constraint. Sometimes, these do lead to out-of-the box thinking and emergence of acceptable middle-ground solutions. More importantly, these meetings do provide excellent opportunities for (a) getting better understanding of past events in the right perspective and (b) quietly exchanging some key messages that could help reduce tension/misunderstanding.

While evaluating the efficacy or otherwise of Track-II engagements in

Indo-Pak relations, it is important to recognize the inherent limitations of the process as mentioned above. Montville had emphasized that Track-Two Diplomacy is not a substitute for Track-One Diplomacy, but compensates for the constraints imposed on leaders by their people's psychological expectations. Most importantly, Track-II Diplomacy is intended to provide a bridge or complement official Track-One negotiations.[6] So, basically Track-II does not drive its own programme or agenda; it only acts as a facilitator or a bridge.

Back Channel vs Track-II

It is important to clarify here that Track-II and Back Channel diplomacy are not synonymous; in fact they refer to two entirely different modes of engagement between countries, may be for the same or similar objectives as Track-I diplomacy through normal diplomatic and political engagements between governments.

In my own limited experience of involvement in both Back Channel and Track-II processes, the differences were quite stark. Back Channel negotiations are conducted in complete secrecy, involve trusted emissaries carrying clear instructions on the agenda, objectives and scope of discussions. These interactions are in aid of Track-I diplomacy, aimed at smoothening negotiations on sensitive aspects of the relations, in the comfort of full deniability. The Vajpayee-Musharraf joint statement of January 6, 2004 is often cited by experts as a classic case of successful Back Channel diplomacy between the key interlocutors (Brajesh Mishra and Tariq Aziz) designated by their leaders and facilitated by a number of key enablers who secretly negotiated various aspects of the deal.

Normally, 'agreements' arrived at by such initiatives have a limited shelf-life, by and large, concurrent with the tenures of the principals. So, it was apprehended that with the unexpected fall of the Vajpayee government in the May 2004 Lok Sabha elections, the ongoing Back Channel diplomacy too would terminate. But this did not happen. The UPA government led by Dr. Manmohan Singh decided to continue with the dialogue with greater vigour between his NSA, Mani Dixit, and Musharraf's representative, Tariq Aziz. Later, after the sudden demise of Dixit in early January 2005, Amb. Sati Lamba took over the role of interlocutor in the Track-II dialogue (or was it Track 1.5?) with Pakistan.

This phase too was very productive with commentators describing 2005 as the 'golden year' of improved bilateral relations. According to both sides, by 2007/8 the interlocutors had nearly 'sealed a deal' with only a few unresolved issues. While Amb. Lamba and Tariq Aziz have not been very enthusiastic about publicly sharing the details of issues agreed upon, former Pakistan Foreign Minister Khurshid Mahmud Kasuri has spelt out many details in his book *'Neither Hawk nor Dove: An Insider's Account of Pakistan's Foreign Policy'* (Viking).[7]

The 'agreements' arrived at through all these efforts and initiatives under Track-1.5 aided by Back Channel efforts, were certainly path-breaking, if one were to go by Kasuri's account. However, as an analyst, one cannot comment on the substantive aspects until both sides decide to put the details in public domain. That does not seem likely.

The developments narrated above, however, confirm the widely-held view that such secret Back Channel negotiations, unless conclusively translated into official agreements, will always suffer from two major disadvantages, namely, (a) absence of validated record of agreements; and (b) low shelf-life; being forgotten as soon as the principals change. This is what possibly happened with the Aziz-Lamba dialogue after Gen. Musharraf was dethroned in Pakistan and on the Indian side, the intense public outrage over the 26/11 (2008) Mumbai carnage perpetrated by LeT militants at ISI's behest, completely wiped out any possibility of continued dialogue at any level and under any format other that Track-II.

As against the afore-mentioned instances of Back Channel efforts, under the Track-II formulation, the participants are largely well-informed and experienced non-elite subject experts carrying no or very limited 'instructions' from their principals. Discussions are not 'secret' but mostly held under Chatham House rules. Recommendations of Track-II meets are generally shared with the policy makers but rarely factored into policy formulations to the extent one would wish. These inputs, even if used, are certainly very rarely so acknowledged.

In comparison, therefore, strategic analysts largely favour a 'Track-1.5' formulation under which some degree of 'instructions' are carried out by some selected participants for seeking reactions and responses and hence more effective in policy formulation processes.

An essential aspect of both the Back Channel and Track-1.5 processes is the secrecy of negotiations. The purists of diplomatic engagements (Track-I) strongly believe that in any free, open democratic society, there should be no room for 'secret' understandings. This is a laudable approach, yet given the growing complexities of bilateral relations, especially in the India-Pakistan context, 'secrecy' of the means employed to arrive at 'understandings' is almost inescapable.

What then can Work in the Current Scenario?

As can be seen from the foregoing discussions, Track-II interactions at different times with different sponsors and different sets of interlocutors, have played an important but a fairly limited role in dealing with the entire gamut of existing and evolving, but always extremely complex, problems define our bilateral relations over the past 72 years since independence. Some of the key issues can be listed here to remind the readers that it is not only confined to huge divergence of positions on Kashmir and trans-border terrorism. Even the so called 'low hanging fruits' like Sir Creek, Siachen, water-sharing are as complex as any and will defy easy and early resolution. Taken together with other issues like bilateral trade, MFN status, visas for easy travel, visits to places of worship, regional cooperation, trade and travel access and connectivity, etc., the challenges are rather formidable.

The fundamental question confounding strategic experts is whether, in the complex situation described above, any of the informal modes of engagement like Track-II or Track-1.5 or even Back Channel have any relevance? Can any of these, individually or in combination, make a difference in reducing tension and in generating better understanding beyond what Track-I (normal diplomacy under direct G2G framework) can achieve?

In this context it would be pertinent to mention that the alternative or additional channels of informal exchange of views and perceptions, have been functioning effectively and making significant contribution even between countries having robust G2G relations like say the USA and UK, USA-Japan and USA-West Europe. Think-tank backed Track-II initiatives between allies are known to provide critical inputs to the policy-making bodies in these countries. Similarly, close allies are also known to maintain robust Back Channel interactions, not only for sharing critical intelligence but equally importantly, to fine-tune their policy options. It is also important to recognise that even between non-alliance countries with excellent political and diplomatic relations, alternative modes are required and they function without any conflict.

In the India-Pakistan context, high-level political contacts are weak and intermittent or mostly remain suspended. Currently, over the last three years, there has been none at the bilateral level and none even during multilateral meets. It is totally frozen. That has naturally affected even normal interactions at the Track-I diplomatic level that can be best described as cold/non-existent or inconsequential.

This is when the need for an alternative channel of communication, all or any of the three, namely, Back Channel, Track-1.5 and/or Track-II, is most critically felt. It can make a difference since the going has indeed become tough. In my view, looking at the complexity of the situation, Track-II can have a very limited impact, if any, since it cannot provide a breakthrough. The need of the hour is to devise a mechanism that can provide the big push. That can come ideally through a direct bold move by the two heads of governments; very unlikely in the present scenario. 'Extending a hand of friendship' in Vajpayee style is unthinkable in today's context. The other workable route could be a major Back Channel push. But for these, the right time can come only after the completion of the ongoing Parliamentary elections in India and formation of a new government with a fresh mandate. That can set the stage rolling once again, with the initial moves coming through Track-I (normal diplomatic channel) contacts, followed by a strong push through Back Channel contacts at a sufficiently high level but, essentially, with a clear agenda.

On the question of agenda, in my view, from the Indian perspective, there should be no going back on the oft-stated position of 'Terror and Talks' not going together. There should be a clear reiteration of the commitments made in the January 6, 2004 Musharraf-Vajpayee joint statement. Terror must end before any meaningful dialogue can commence. Obviously, the agenda must include the prime concerns of both the countries; end of trans-border terror for India and the Kashmir issue for Pakistan. If this approach is not adhered to, the gains of years of 'hard work' will become a wasteful exercise, making the whole process infructuous.

If one were to go by what Kasuri and Sati Lamba have stated publicly, a lot can be achieved. In fact, the 'agreements' then arrived at could well be the starting point for future discussions rather than reinventing the wheel all over again. The Track-II dialogue can then regain its relevance and momentum only through a graded approach as suggested above. It can contribute immensely by debating various options and suggesting answers to seemingly intractable questions.

NOTES

1. McDonald, John W. and Daine B. Bendahmane, *Conflict Resolution: Track Two Diplomacy*, Foreign Service Institute, US Department of State, 1987.
2. Davidson, William D. and Joseph V. Monteville. "Foreign Policy According to Freud", *Foreign Policy*, No. 45, Winter 1981-82, pp. 145-57.
3. McDonald, John W. and Daine B. Bendahmane, *Conflict Resolution: Track Two Diplomacy*. Foreign Service Institute, US Department of State, 1987, p. 10.
4. Ambassador G. Parthasarthy had written in *Advancing India's Conversation with the World*, for the Ministry of External Affairs's Public Policy Division, December 24, 2010.
5. Back Channel diplomacy refers to secret lines of communication held open between two adversaries. It is often communicated through an informal intermediary or through a third party.
6. Jeffery Mapendere, 'Track One and a Half Diplomacy and the Complementarity of Tracks', *Culture of Peace Online Journal*, 2(1), 2000, pp. 66-81. Available from: https://peacemaker.un.org/sites/peacemaker.un.org/files/TrackOneandaHalfDiplomacy_Mapendere.pdf
7. Khurshid Mahmud Kasuri, *Neither a Hawk nor a Dove: An Insider's Account of Pakistan's Foreign Policy*, Oxford University Press, Oxford, 2015.

15

Balakote and Its Aftermath: Analysing Pakistan's Strategic Elite Response

Brig. Rahul Bhonsle (Retd)

Introduction

This article attempts a descriptive analysis of the response of the Pakistan state elite to the pre-emptive air strike by the Indian Air Force on 26 February 2019 at Balakote, training camp of the internationally-proscribed terrorist group Jaish-e-Mohammad, to provide markers for possible reactions in a similar dynamic in the future. Given the tortuous history of India-Pakistan relations, to assume that Balakote is the last skirmish witnessed between armed forces of the two sides may be fallacious. Against the backdrop of possession of weapons of mass destruction by India and Pakistan, there is a need to analyse response in times of conflict to ensure escalation controls are exercised to prevent consequences arising from miscommunications on either side. Elite response in similar circumstances examined rigorously may provide some guidance. Briefly, Pakistan's strategic elite displayed consistency in denial [of support to terrorism in Kashmir & impact of Indian air strikes], justification [indirect support to terror], deflection [India's reaction as a ploy to garner votes for general elections], lack of empathy [towards the victims of terror], victimhood [of Pak to terror for decades] and, expectedly, nationalism and unity. A word of caution, there are inherent advantages and problems in reviewing an incident in the immediate aftermath such as recall and inadequacy of evidence, respectively, which could be factored in by the reader.

Backdrop to Balakote

On 14 February, a vehicle-borne improvised explosive device (VBIED) attack was carried out by a terrorist cadre of the Jaish-e-Mohammad (JeM) on a convoy of the Central Reserve Police Force (CRPF) in Pulwama, Kashmir that caused immediate fatal casualties to over 40 police personnel and injured several others. The JeM almost immediately claimed the attack after floating a video of the terrorist on social media. India's Prime Minister, Mr. Narendra Modi, while condemning the incident and empathising with the martyrs, tweeted that "a befitting reply will be given to the perpetrators of the heinous attack and their patrons."[1] In the same vein, Prime Minister Modi on another occasion, inaugurating the high-speed Vande Bharat Express between New Delhi and Varanasi from New Delhi Railway Station on 15 February said, "We have given full freedom to the security forces.... I want to tell the terror outfits and those aiding and abetting them that they have made a big mistake. They will have to pay a very heavy price for their actions...Let me assure the nation that those behind this attack, the perpetrators of this attack, will be punished."[2]

On 26 February, an Indian Air Force (IAF) Mirage 2000 fighter mission carried out a pre-emptive air strike on the JeM terrorist training camp between 3:45 a.m. and 4:04 a.m. Indian Standard Time at Balakote in Khyber Pakhtunkhwa (KPK) province in Pakistan. Spice 2000 precision laser-guided bombs, each weighing over 1,000 kg, were used to target the facility with pinpoint accuracy. The target, Jaba Top, in Balakot was selected based on specific information of a large number of cadres of the JeM at the site and the standoff distance from civilian area to prevent non-terrorist casualties.

Briefing the media, Indian Foreign Secretary Mr. Vijay Keshav Gokhale outlined that this was, "an intelligence-led operation in the early hours of today [26 February], India struck the biggest training camp of JeM in Balakot. In this operation, a very large number of JeM terrorists, trainers, senior commanders and groups of jihadis who were being trained for fidayeen action were eliminated. This facility at Balakot was headed by Maulana Yousuf Azhar (alias Ustad Ghouri), the brother-in-law of Masood Azhar, Chief of JeM".[3] Pakistan denied the existence of a terrorist camp in Balakote and the impact of the air strike.

A day after, on 27 February, Pakistan claimed that the Pakistan Air Force (PAF) had carried out air strikes across the Line of Control to demonstrate its "right, will and capability for self defence."[4] In the aerial skirmish, an Indian pilot, Wing Commander Abhinandan Varthaman, flying a MiG-21 Bison fighter had to eject and landed in Pakistan-Occupied Jammu and Kashmir (POJK) and was taken a prisoner of war (POW). Pakistan attempted to make much of the captivity of the pilot and released videos to which India objected and demanded the immediate release of the pilot. On 28 February, Pakistan Prime Minister Imran Khan intimated to the parliament that Indian Wing Commander would be released and on 1 March he was handed over at the Wagah border crossing between the two countries, near Amritsar.

Tensions between the two sides continued with a high state of readiness of the armed forces, particularly the Air Force, for weeks leading Pakistan to place restrictions on overflight of airspace amongst other measures. However, by the middle of March as general elections were announced in India, the focus shifted in-country in New Delhi. For the main objective of the article, this short sequence of events is considered adequate.

Defining Pakistan's Elite

In consideration of the subject under discussion defining Pakistan's strategic elites assumes importance as key decisions on national security are made by this select body and the group varies from state to state. In Pakistan, the National Security Committee (NSC) headed by the Prime Minister, is the apex strategic decision-making body. However, the dominant role and influence of the Pakistan Army in the decision hierarchy is well established. The Army Chief, apart from other Services chiefs and Chairman Joint Chiefs of Staff, is a part of the NSC.

Army decisions are made in the collegial body of Corps Commanders—three-star generals who head the nine corps[5] in Pakistan. Periodic Corps Commanders conferences are held, chaired by the Chief of Staff of the Pakistan Army, to adopt key policies. Thus, the armed forces in general apart from the influence in the NSC play a critical role. While this may appear to be a closed loop of sorts for strategic decision-making, the Pakistan parliament—the National Assembly in particular apart from the Senate—are influencing factors. The weak government led by the ruling party, Pakistan Tehreek Insaaf of Prime Minister Imran Khan, necessitated that Parliament be taken into confidence.

Importantly, the civil society of Pakistan, more particularly the media, has limited, if any, weight in strategic decision-making though vernacular Urdu papers are supportive of groups such as the Lashkar-e-Taiyyaba (LeT) and the Jaish-e-Mohammad (JeM) and their role in fostering terrorism in

J&K and India. How far this is a sentiment from the ground and how this is manipulated, however, is difficult to discern. The armed forces Director-General Inter-Services Public Relations (DGISPR) has extensive control over the media which is evident from recent restrictions on military veterans who can appear on television shows in the country. Statements by the DGISPR also carry weight.

Amongst the ministries, the Ministry of Foreign Affairs led by veteran foreign minister Shah Mahmood Qureshi, assumes importance while the Ministry of Defence is subsumed by the decisions taken by the Pakistan Army General Hqs and has virtually no role to play. Examining the response of Prime Minister (PM) Imran Khan, the NCA, the PM-Army Chief interaction, DGISPR reactions, Ministry of Foreign Affairs and parliamentary discourse is thus considered necessary for the stated purpose of the article.

Examining Elite Response

Post Pulwama

The first official reaction from Pakistan on the Pulwama terrorist attack was on 14 February the day of the incident. The Pakistan Ministry of Foreign Affairs stated, "The attack in Pulwama in the Indian Occupied Jammu & Kashmir is a matter of grave concern. We have always condemned heightened acts of violence in the Valley. We strongly reject any insinuation by elements in the Indian government and media circles that seek to link the attack to the State of Pakistan without investigations."[6]

As a consequence of statements from the Indian Ministry of External Affairs and other sources which categorically indicated the involvement of the Pakistan-based terrorist group, the JeM, the Pakistan Ministry of Foreign Affairs issued a detailed statement on 17 February.[7] The following major points were stated (1) Pakistan rejected Indian allegations as these were made immediately after the attack and without investigations. These were stated to be, "knee-jerk and pre-conceived accusations that were nevertheless consistent with well-rehearsed tactics from Indian playbook after such incidents in the past"; (2) JeM is a proscribed entity in Pakistan since 2002; (3) Indian claims were based on social media inputs [video released by JeM immediately after the attack; (4) Indian security and Intelligence lapses led to the attack; (5) Pak desire to normalise relations with India and measures taken thereof; and (6) Linked the Indian response to internal political interests.[8]

On 18 February, Pakistan's Foreign Minister Mr Shah Mahmood Qureshi wrote a letter to the UN Secretary-General which highlighted the deteriorating security situation in the region with threat of use of force against Pakistan by India and claimed that India ascribing the Pulwama attack to Pakistan was "absurd," while tensions were being ratcheted up for domestic reasons and demanded de-escalation.[9]

On 19 February, Prime Minister Imran Khan addressed the nation on the Pulwama attack after the visit of the Crown Prince of Saudi Arabia and the Investment Conference by which time tensions had ratcheted up. Khan reiterated the points made by the Foreign Office, i.e., lack of evidence, denial of involvement of Pakistan, especially in the wake of the visit of the Crown Prince of Saudi Arabia, Pakistan's own losses as a victim of terror, India's continued inaction to resolve the Kashmir dispute and to engage in a dialogue with Pakistan. He also reiterated the cliché that "Naya Pakistan," will not be used for the conduct of terrorist attacks on neighbours, indicated a willingness for investigations based on evidence provided by India, made an offer of dialogue and bracketed Indian reaction to sloganeering for elections. He also warned that Pakistan will retaliate if attacked and that the consequences of war were indeterminable.[10]

Pakistan convened a meeting of the NSC at the Prime Minister's Office on 21 February chaired by Mr Imran Khan. The NSC, as expected, stated, "the state of Pakistan is not involved in any way, means or form in the said [Pulwama] incident" and that it was "conceived, planned and executed indigenously." An offer was made to India for dialogue. "We expect India to positively respond to the offers," it added and Pakistan "shall take action against anyone found using our soil [for terrorism]". The NSC statement went on to counsel India to carry out, "deep introspection to realise why [the] people of Indian-occupied Kashmir have lost [the] fear of death". "The violence by Indian forces in Indian-occupied Kashmir is highly counterproductive. The global community needs to play its part in resolving the long-pending Kashmir issue in accordance with UN resolutions and aspirations of the Kashmiris."[11,12] The statement also indicated that Prime Minister Imran Khan had authorised the armed forces of Pakistan to respond 'decisively' and 'comprehensively' to any aggression or misadventure by India. "This is Naya Pakistan...and we are determined to demonstrate to our people that the State is capable of protecting them...we believe that the monopoly of violence stays with the State only,"

Prime Minister Imran Khan was quoted.[13] A copy of the statement of the NCA was forwarded to the President of the United Nations Security Council.

A statement issued by Pakistan's Interior Ministry indicated that the federal government had imposed a ban on the Jammat-ud-Dawa (JuD) and the so-called humanitarian arm of the terrorist group, Falah-e-Insaniat Foundation (FIF). "It has been decided that the Jamaat-ud-Dawa and the Falah-e-Insaniat Foundation be notified as proscribed organisations," the statement said.[14] Importantly these directions came after the February 2018 Ordinance proscribing the group had lapsed. The Supreme Court of Pakistan in September 2018 permitted the two organisations to continue their relief and charity work in the country. No concrete action on the JeM was however outlined.

On 22 February, Foreign Minister Shah Mahmood Qureshi wrote to the President of the United Nations Security Council (UNSC) to draw attention to "the deteriorating security situation in our region resulting from Indian belligerence and threats of use of force against Pakistan. The situation poses a threat to international peace and security." The same arguments were made of lack of evidence pointing to Pakistan, failure of Indian security, domestic political compulsions of New Delhi, threats by Indian leaders of retaliation and offer of talks and investigations by Pakistan to India. Threat of abrogation of the Indus Waters Treaty (IWT) was added. In a way, the letter also seemed to accept Pakistan's role in fostering terrorism in Jammu and Kashmir as it stated that "India continues a motivated propaganda campaign to portray the legitimate Kashmiri struggle for self-determination as "terrorism.""[15]

The Pakistan National Assembly unanimously passed a resolution strongly rejecting what it called, "baseless Indian allegations" that sought to link Pakistan—without an investigation and "any shred of evidence"—to the Pulwama attack.

Responding to the statements from India and also the measures taken by New Delhi such as issuing diplomatic demarche to many countries to isolate Pakistan, the Foreign Ministry in Islamabad established a crisis management cell. Discussions were held with former diplomats on the approach to be adopted and members of the diplomatic corps in Islamabad were kept in the loop.

Response of the Armed Forces

Given statements by the Indian Prime Minister, Mr Narendra Modi, and other leaders, Pakistan could be said to have been forewarned of impeding military action by the Indian armed forces. There were also sufficient indications that a land-based surgical strike or a deep penetration raid that was undertaken by the Special Forces of the Indian Army after the terrorist attack in Uri in 2016 will not be the course adopted. A cross-border air strike was possibly visualised as one of the options. Thus, Chief of the Air Staff Air Chief Marshal Mujahid Anwar Khan stated on 25 February that the Pakistan Air Force (PAF) would "thwart any misadventure by the enemy" while he visited the forward operating airbases of the air force. He was quoted as saying that Pakistan was a "peace-loving nation" but warned that "if the war is imposed on us, we would defend the aerial frontiers of our motherland at any cost."[16] Ominously, the Indian Air Force strike at Balakote happened the same night (25/26 February).

Response to Balakote Air Strike

Initial Response

As indicated, the Indian Air Force carried out the air strike at Balakote penetrating Pakistan air space in the night of 25/26 February. The first reaction from Pakistan and indeed from both sides was a series of tweets by the DG ISPR early morning on 26 February. The first tweet was "Indian Air Force violated Line of Control. Pakistan Air Force immediately scrambled. Indian aircrafts gone back. Details to follow.[17] In a second tweet, the DG ISPR stated that Indian aircraft intruded from Muzafarabad sector. Facing timely and effective response from the Pakistan Air Force it released its payload in haste while escaping which fell near Balakot. No casualties or damage.[18] There was a long gap after a series of tweets that indicate a sense of shock and disbelief possibly that the Indians could carry out their bluff and that Pakistan's airspace could be penetrated, this too for the second time in recent years, the first being the raid by American Special Forces to take out al-Qaeda chief Osama Bin Laden in 2011.

Responses from the Foreign Office

The Pakistan Foreign Office summoned the Acting High Commissioner of India as the High Commissioner, Ajay Bisaria, had been recalled to Delhi for consultations the same day—for lodging a protest. The statement from the Pakistan Ministry of Foreign Affairs indicated that the "Acting Foreign Secretary summoned the Indian Acting High Commissioner and strongly condemned the Indian violation of Pakistan's sovereignty and territorial integrity when at approximately 0254 hours today, 8 Indian aircraft were effectively intercepted by Pakistani Air Force jets and forced to scuttle back, while randomly releasing their ordnance which landed in an uninhabited remote area. Baseless, reprehensible Indian claims of targeting a large terrorist camp and resultant casualties to placate Indian domestic audience and electioneering were strongly rebutted". The statement indicated that Pakistan will give, "a befitting response at a time and place of its choosing." Pakistan's non-involvement in the Pulwama terrorist attack was reiterated.[19]

On the same day, the Foreign Minister, Shah Mahmood Qureshi, briefed the diplomatic corps on the Indian strike at Balakote to highlight "Indian violation of Pakistan's sovereignty and territorial integrity," and went on with the rebuttal of Pak involvement in Pulwama and a right to retaliate. The Foreign Minister claimed, "Pakistan's principled stance on continuing support to the peaceful political struggle of the Kashmiri people for the realization of the right to self-determination as enshrined in the UN Security Council Resolutions."[20]

Military Reactions

On 26 February, Chief of Army Staff, General Qamar Javed Bajwa and Chief of Air Staff, Air Chief Marshal Mujahid Anwar Khan, held a joint meeting at the Air HQ. Importantly, the Army Chief visited the Air HQ despite the perception that the Army is the dominant service in Pakistan, thus an outreach was evident. ISPR also claimed that "Pakistan Army troops are at high alert along the Line of Control (LoC) with all required safeguards along Eastern Border in place to thwart any Indian aggression." "During the last 48 hours, Indian troops have resorted to increased ceasefire violations in Kotli, Khuiratta and Tatta Pani Sectors along LoC. Pakistan Army troops responding effectively," the statement added. "Reports of casualties to Indian forces and damage to Indian posts. Indian deliberate firing on civilians has resulted in martyrdom of four citizens and two [citizens] injured." "Pakistan's armed forces are in a state of readiness for all eventualities," the statement added. "The public to stay mindful of rumour mills and stay responsible in the use of social media," it cautioned.[21] A defensive posture on the LoC and preparations for a strike seem to have been made on this day.

Pak Riposte

Initial Statement

On 27 February, as per the Pakistan Ministry of Foreign Affairs, "Pakistan Air

Force undertook strikes across Line of Control from within Pakistani airspace," thus attempting to convey that violation of Indian air space had not taken place, the targets engaged were non military, human loss and collateral damage was avoided and the purpose was to, "demonstrate our right, will and capability for self defence. We have no intention of escalation, but are fully prepared to do so if forced into that paradigm." The statement also claimed that, "India is striking at so-called terrorist backers without a shred of evidence, we also retain reciprocal rights to retaliate against elements that enjoy Indian patronage while carrying out acts of terror in Pakistan."[22] The subtle play of words in the factually incorrect statement attempted to convey that as the Line of Control had not been crossed, Pakistan had not violated Indian air space and thus attempted to place the onus on India for escalation. The fact that the PAF did not have ground attack standoff weapons that could accurately avoid 'military' targets was conveniently overlooked.

The DGISPR Maj Gen Asif Ghafoor highlighted the reaction to the Indian Air Force's actions to defend air space as an offensive manoeuvre. He tweeted, "In response to PAF strikes this morning as released by MoFA, IAF crossed LOC. PAF shot down two Indian aircrafts inside Pakistani airspace. One of the aircraft fell inside AJ&K while other fell inside IOK. One Indian pilot arrested by troops on ground while two in the area.[23] While the Indian MiG-21 Bison pilot was held as a PoW, the mystery of the second aircraft has remained unresolved with the IAF indicating that this was a PAF F-16 with the precise location of the fall having been released recently.

On the same day, [27 February], Prime Minister Imran Khan addressed the nation to reiterate his message of peace and offer for dialogue. "I ask India: with the weapons you have and the weapons we have, can we really afford such a miscalculation? If this escalates, things will no longer be in my control or in Modi's," the Prime Minister said. "I once again invite you: we are ready. We understand the grief India has suffered in Pulwama and are ready for any sort of dialogue on terrorism. I reiterate that better sense should prevail. Let's sit together and settle this with talks," the Prime Minister concluded.[24]

A joint session of the Pakistan Parliament was held on 28 February to discuss rising tension with India in the wake of the Pulwama attack and subsequent airstrikes by both countries. Prime Minister Imran Khan thanked the opposition for standing by the government "at a time when Pakistan is facing an external threat." "We realised that it was because of upcoming elections in India," he said and added that the government decided to wait until the polls in India were over before making another offer for talks. However, he disclosed he had "feared they (India) would do something." "We realised that Pakistani people might get upset that we did not respond, but we (*army chief and premier*[25]) decided that since we did not know if there were any casualties, in case of an immediate response there will be escalation." "Do not take this confrontation further," the Pakistan Prime Minister said as quoted by the media, addressing the Indian leadership. "In our desire for peace, I announce that tomorrow, and as a first step to open negotiations, Pakistan will be releasing the Indian Air Force officer in our custody," PM Khan said.[26] The pilot was subsequently released on 1 March 2019.[27]

On 2 March, the Pakistan Ministry of Foreign Affairs released the details of the resolution passed by the parliament joint session indicating the response of the elected representatives:[28] While most of the points made at various times during the series of encounters have been reiterated, these may be worth a recall as a summary and included condemnation of what was called India's, "aggression of 26 and 27 February 2019,' dismissing claims of destruction of terrorists' facility, lauding timely and effective action by the PAF which claimed to have repulsed the Indian attack without loss of life or property even though it was openly accepted even by Pakistan's Defence Minister that the PAF could not discover the Indian air penetration as it was, "night". The resolution dismissing Indian allegations claimed that this was "guided by its [India's] electoral calculations' and ironically offered "Pakistan's assistance to India in investigations of the Pulwama attack and to take action on actionable intelligence or evidence."[29]

Summary of Conclusions on Pak Elite Responses

As is evident from the recount of responses in Pakistan to Pulwama, Balakote and the aerial skirmish, there is consistency in denial, deflection and blame-shifting across the board by the elite in perfect unison. The narrative between the Prime Minister, Foreign Minister, Foreign Office and the DGISPR remains the same. However, DGISPR faltered a number of times possibly in the urge to trigger a favourable news cycle by giving the lead to the media and others. A lack of empathy to loss of lives in a major terrorist incident on an unarmed convoy of CRPF was notable. The denial included the Pakistan state and the terrorist group, JeM's, involvement in the Pulwama terrorist attack in J&K, refutation of JeM losses in the Balakote air strike as well as the loss of F-16 fighter aircraft and pilot in the skirmish on 27 February. The deep penetration of Pakistan air space by the IAF was denoted as a minor infringement. In addition, the denial of the PAF penetration of the LoC on 27 February by claiming that it remained in Pak airspace was also evident.

Obfuscation of continued support to the JeM and other terrorist groups with only token action against the JuD and FIF which may be a response to the commitments required for avoiding black listing by the Financial Action Task Force (FATF) is also evident. However in a Freudian slip, Pakistan's otherwise suave and experienced Foreign Minister Shah Mahmood Qureshi accepted in an interview to the *BBC* that he knew JeM was not involved in the terror attack in Pulwama as they had been asked about it, thus indicating that the government was in touch with the terrorist group.[30]

Deflection of the reason for the Indian response on Balakote which was indicated as creating a facade for the purposes of the general elections rather than the deep trauma that was suffered by the nation and especially the families who lost their breadwinners was ignored. This lack of empathy towards victims is striking and is one of the roots for Pakistan's sustained use of terror as a tool for instability in the neighbourhood. This is possibly also a reason why the strategic elite firewalled from terror within Pakistan has repeatedly compromised with extremists and has failed to eliminate the roots of violent extremism within the country.

Continued overt support to separatism in Kashmir where the blame is placed solely on India and reading between the lines support to terrorists designated as, "freedom fighters", a traditional policy of Pakistan is evident and there is unlikely to be any change in the near future. Indirectly, this has been used as a justification of Pakistan's support to terrorism in Kashmir while an attempt is made to shield this support by claiming that a country which is one of the biggest victims of terror could not be a supporter of the same. Pakistan's logic that a victim of terror cannot support terrorism in Kashmir has been frequently quoted by the country's leadership including the military. The Pulwama terror attack indicates the irony behind this verbal subterfuge and supporters of Pakistan in the international community who have accepted this spin blindly need to be explained these falsehoods.

Internationalisation of the issue by alleging Indian belligerence and painting Pakistan as a "dove" looking for regional peace and stability was flouted indicating that there was no change in the approach while Prime Minister Khan claimed that he had reached out to the Indian leadership. The facade of willingness to investigate based on evidence was shed early as on 27 March

2019 when Pakistan rejected the dossier provided by India containing evidence on involvement of the JeM in the Pulwama attack.[31]

Nationalism and unity in support of the armed forces were not unexpected given the need of the hour; however, absence of a debate for revoking terror as an instrument of state policy has been muted and mainly in the Pak media.[32] Finally, the closed loop decision-making at the apex—Army Chief and Prime Minister—is evident with Mr. Khan's statement in the parliament. In the end, it will be fruitful to recall the saying—the more things change, the more they remain the same even if it is the so-called Naya Pakistan.

NOTES

1. Prime Minister's Address, A befitting reply will be given to the perpetrators of the heinous attack and their patrons: PM, https://www.youtube.com/watch?v=7EH2D3qOrPY [Accessed April 14, 2019].
2. "Terrorists will pay a heavy price for Pulwama attack: Modi", *The Hindu*, Chennai, February 15, 2019.
3. "Statement by Foreign Secretary on 26 February 2019 on the Strike on JeM training camp at Balakot", at https://www.mea.gov.in/press-releases.htm?dtl/31091/Statement_by_Foreign_Secretary_on_26_February_2019_on_the_Strike_on_JeM_training_camp_at_Balakot [Accessed April 15, 2019].
4. "Pakistan strikes back", at http://www.mofa.gov.pk/pr-details.php [Accessed April 14, 2019].
5. Pakistan corps is a composite theatre level formation comprising of a varied number of armoured and infantry divisions with supporting arms and services having a degree of independence in terms of operational conduct in times of war and administrative controls in a no-war scenario.
6. "Attack in Pulwama", at http://www.mofa.gov.pk/pr-details.php [Accessed April 15, 2019].
7. "India's Pursuit of Self-Serving Narrative on Pulwama Attack", at http://www.mofa.gov.pk/pr-details.php [Accessed April 15, 2019].
8. Ibid.
   "Foreign Minister's letter to UN Secretary General", at http://www.mofa.gov.pk/pr-details.php. [accessed April 15, 2019].
9. "Prime Minister Imran Khan's address on Pulwama Incident", at http://www.mofa.gov.pk/pr-details.php [accessed April 15, 2019].
10. "PM Khan authorises army to respond to any aggression, misadventure by India", at https://www.geo.tv/latest/228816-fo-officials-brief-nsc-on-kulbhushan-jadhav-case-hearing-sources [Accessed April 15, 2019].
11. Sanaullah Khan, "NSC orders acceleration of anti-terrorism ops", *Dawn*, Islamabad, February 21, 2019.
12. Staff Report, "Army authorised to respond to any Indian misadventure", *Daily Times*, Lahore, June 19, 2019.
13. Ibid.

14. "Foreign Minister writes to President UN Security Council (UNSC)" at http://www.mofa.gov.pk/pr-details.php [Accessed April 15, 2019].
15. "PAF ready to 'thwart any misadventure by the enemy, says air chief", *Dawn*, Islamabad, June 19, 2019.
16. Tweet by Maj Gen Asif Ghafoor Verified account @OfficialDGISPR. Available at https://twitter.com/OfficialDGISPR/status/1100179216375693318. [Accessed 15 April 2019].
17. Tweet by Maj Gen Asif Ghafoor Verified account @OfficialDGISPR, at https://twitter.com/OfficialDGISPR/status/1100207947022565377 [Accessed 15 April 15, 2019].
18. "Pakistan strongly protests Indian aggression, violation of its airspace and promises a befitting response", at http://www.mofa.gov.pk/pr-details.php [Accessed April 15, 2019].
19. "Foreign Minister Briefs the Diplomatic Corps on Intrusion by Indian Aircraft on 26th February, 2019", at http://www.mofa.gov.pk/pr-details.php [Accessed 15 April 2019].
20. "Pakistan's armed forces on high alert, ready for any", *Dawn*, Islamabad, February 28, 2019.
21. "Pakistan Strikes Back", at www.mofa.gov.pk/pr-details.php [Accessed April 15,2019].
22. Tweet by Maj Gen Asif Ghafoor Verified account @OfficialDGISPR, at https://twitter.com/OfficialDGISPR/status/1100641491679150080 [Accessed April 15, 2019].
23. "Video: Wing Commander Abhinandan says Pakistani Army treated him with respect", at https://www.dawn.com/news/1466413 [Accessed April 15, 2019].
24. Italics by author to highlight the role of Army Chief in decision making in Pakistan.
25. "Do not escalate this further, PM Khan warns India during joint session of Parliament", *Dawn*, Islamabad, February 28, 2019.
26. "Return of Indian POW, Wing Commander Abhinandan Varthaman", at http://www.mofa.gov.pk/pr-details.php [Accessed 15 April 2019]
27. "Resolution Passed By The Majlis-E-Shoora (Parliament) In Joint Sitting", at http://www.mofa.gov.pk/pr-details.php. [Accessed 15 April 2019].
28. Ibid.
29. "Watch: Pak Foreign Minister Fumbles When Asked About Contact With Jaish" at NDTV https://www.ndtv.com/india-news/pulwama-terror-attack-pakistan-foreign-minister-shah-mehmood-qureshi-fumbles-when-asked-about-contac-2001747. [Accessed April 15, 2019].
30. "Pakistan Rejects India's Pulwama Dossier" at https://www.security-risks.com/security-trends-south-asia/pakistan/pakistan-rejects-india%E2%80%99s-pulwama-dossier-13012.html. [Accessed April 15, 2019].
31. "Pakistan Media Calls for Action Against Jaish, Abdicating Terrorist Groups," at https://www.security-risks.com/security-trends-south-asia/pakistan/pakistan-media-calls-for-action-against-jaish-abdicating-terrorist-groups-12975.html. [Accessed April 15, 2019].

16

Gilgit-Baltistan: Unclear Road to Political Reforms

Prateek Joshi

Introduction

Though the occupied region of Gilgit-Baltistan (GB) remains at the centre of the Kashmir issue, it came into the headlines after the China Pakistan Economic Corridor (CPEC) was unveiled in 2015. Since the corridor links China and Pakistan via GB, protests by the Indian foreign office gave Islamabad further impetus to work towards defining its political relationship with Pakistan on clearer lines, given the absence of the GB's representation in the federal structure. In late 2015, the government formed a committee under leadership of the then National Security Advisor, Sartaj Aziz, to suggest potential political reforms to empower GB's residents. The political situation in the GB seemed normal until November 2017, which marked the beginning of a sensitive phase. From widespread protests against imposition of taxes, to the promulgation of the Gilgit Baltistan Order, 2018, and finally the Supreme Court (SC) of Pakistan's verdict terming GB as a disputed territory in January 2019, these developments kept the region at the forefront of the political discourse in Pakistan. Besides the Pakistan Army's ongoing efforts at strengthening its hold on the region under the pretext of guarding the CPEC and checking dissent from nationalists, the recent phase has witnessed Pakistan's civilian leadership and judiciary attempting to define the region's political relationship with Pakistan. This article discusses the controversies emerging from Islamabad's attempts at tweaking GB's administrative relationship with

Pakistan in the garb of political reforms, which in turn attracted the apex court's intervention. The article analyses that despite upholding its previous stance of GB being a disputed territory, the SC not only failed to give any direction to the prevailing limbo, but rather ended up restoring the old status-quo that had led to the protests in late 2017.

The Prelude: Protests against Taxes and Abolition of GB Council

The people of GB rose in protest against Islamabad in November 2017 when the Prime Minister-led GB Council announced the imposition of direct taxes on the region under the Income Tax Act (2012).[1] The decision was taken despite the issue of taxation being a bone of contention, given the disputed status of GB. It was a rare instance as protestors (mostly traders and activists) led synchronized agitations across the region, bringing entire GB to a virtual shutdown. The protests also witnessed the revival of the Awami Action Committee—a collection of nearly two dozen religious and nationalist parties—nearly after four years of its formation in 2014 when Islamabad decided to withdraw wheat subsidies from the region.[2] Unlike in the past, when the establishment engineered a split in the movement, the protests continued unabated in the region this time. The agitation did not get any traction from the Pakistani authorities or its media until the Indian media reported on these developments. Although it was the tax order that triggered the protests, the larger demand was granting of province-hood and constitutional rights on par with Pakistani citizens until the Kashmir issue was resolved.

The stage was set for intervention by the civilian establishment which abolished the GB Council, followed by the promulgation of the GB order in May 2018 on the pretext of granting greater rights to the people. In February 2018, the then Prime Minister of Pakistan. Shahid Khaqan Abbasi, announced the abolition of the GB Council, stating that the Council's powers would be transferred to the legislative assembly.[3] The news was received positively by the people of GB as the decision would have paved the way for substantial devolution of powers. The Council's power to legislate on key subjects like forests, minerals and hydropower had long been a source of disquiet between the GB government and Islamabad as the former's jurisdiction had been deliberately kept curtailed by Islamabad.

GB Order, 2018: Controversial Provisions and Judicial Intervention

Soon after, in May, the promulgation of the new GB Order became a source of controversy after some of its provisions were found to be encroaching on the regional autonomy, especially at a time when the Pakistan Muslim League-Nawaz (PML-N)-led government had explicitly promised to transfer the Council's powers to the GB legislative assembly. Prime Minister Abbasi's decision to abolish the GB Council, which initially generated strong hopes among GB's masses, soon turned into despair with the introduction of the new Order. Compared to the GB (Empowerment and Self Governance) Order, 2009, the 2018 Order had certain regressive provisions that sought to exercise greater control over GB. For instance, in the 2009 Order, a "citizen" was defined as "a person who has a domicile of Gilgit-Baltistan," but in the 2018 Order, this definition was changed to person "under the Pakistan citizenship Act (1951)," This raised suspicions that the new provision could be used to legitimize the settlement of outsiders in the region, a long-standing concern of the locals to which Islamabad had never paid any attention. The suspicion has only grown after the inception of CPEC as infrastructure and resource extraction projects are bound to attract labour from outside.

Another new controversial addition was Article 5, which states that "obedience to this Order and law is the inviolable obligation of every citizen," something which clearly points towards the state's efforts at instilling docility in GB's populace. The change in the definition of "citizen" was misinterpreted by Islamabad as bringing the people of GB on par with Pakistani citizens.

The GB Council was abolished in the new Order, but its powers were transferred to the Prime Minister, vesting in him nearly complete autonomy to legislate on key subjects.[4] Article 62 granted "Prime Minister the powers to adopt an amendment in the existing laws or any new law in force subject to the legislative competence," and Article 65 empowered the Prime Minister to levy taxes in GB. Federal bias was also seen in the criteria for selecting the chief judge of the GB Supreme Appellate Court, wherein Article 75(2) states that a "retired judge of the Supreme Court of Pakistan" or a "retired Chief Justice of a High Court" was eligible for the position. To allay the rising local discontent, misleading statements were made by local politicians, wherein GB's law minister wrongly stated that "all powers exercised by the four provincial assemblies under Schedule IV of the Constitution of Pakistan had been entrusted to the GB Assembly."[5] Other promises by Islamabad, like a separate civil service for GB and quota in the Central Superior Service, have not been fulfilled until now.

The controversies surrounding Islamabad's attempts at altering the administrative relationship with GB automatically attracted the judiciary's intervention, which too fell short of addressing the concerns of the people. The SC, besides hearing an old case related to GB's status, also took note of the present controversies and reiterated that GB was a disputed area and called for extending Fundamental Rights to the people in their full capacity. Contrary to the perception that the SC's ruling has stemmed from its concern for the GB's residents, this article shall explain how the ruling came from an altogether different impetus.

It all began with sharp criticism from the existing GB Council members protesting against the PM's decision to abolish the Council. One of the members of the GB Legislative Assembly, who simultaneously held the Council's membership, filed a petition in the Supreme Appellate Court of GB citing that he "took the oath under Article 33 of the GB Empowerment and Self-Governance Order 2009 and was entitled to hold the office till 2020."[6] According to the petitioner, "the new order should not [have been] be introduced till their tenure was completed".[7]

As a result, a stay order was issued by the appellate court against the abolition of the Council on April 24, 2018. Later, in July 2018, the appellate court suspended the new order stating that "despite stay order of the court, GB Order 2018 was introduced, which was in violation of law."[8] In response, the federal government moved the SC against the appellate court's verdict. The SC restored the order in August 2018. Ironically, Pakistan's Chief Justice, Mian Saqib Nisar, remarked that "the order has been restored as people of GB should have the same rights as those in other parts of the country do."[9]

SC Ruling on GB's Status: Strengthening the State's Writ

The SC examined the matter on a fast track basis. In December, it formed a committee headed by the Attorney General "to prepare a final draft of planned reforms for Gilgit-Baltistan".[10] The committee's observations, along with those of the Sartaj Aziz committee became the basis of the Supreme Court's ruling in January 2019.

The ruling was based on three questions, as enumerated ad verbatim in the ruling:[11]

1. Would granting Fundamental Rights within the constitutional scheme of Pakistan prejudice Pakistan's cause for the resolution of the Kashmir 'dispute'?
2. What rights can be granted to the people of Gilgit Baltistan?
3. Is the appellate court a constitutional authority?

The judgment begins by quoting the works by Indian authors S.P. Agarwal (author of *Modern History of Jammu Kashmir: Ancient Times to Shimla Agreement*) and Aman Hingorani (author of *Unravelling the Kashmir Knot*) to substantiate Nehru's commitment towards a plebiscite in Jammu and Kashmir.[12] Without discussing the precondition for a plebiscite—since it calls for Pakistani demilitarisation of the occupied territory—the SC highlighted India's inability to carry out plebiscite as the sole reason for denial of rights to the people of GB. Accepting GB as a 'disputed' territory, the court urged the government to ensure fundamental rights for the people of GB and setting up requisite institutional mechanisms to grant these rights, but in a way, that does not compromise GB's position in the UN. In this way, the SC also claimed to have saved Pakistan from complicating the position of GB in the UN.

A detailed reading of the ruling reveals that there is nothing new in the present judgment. Rather, the court drew extensively from its previous ruling in the 1999 Al-Jehad trust case and only reiterated the recommendations of the Sartaz Aziz Committee. The ruling recalled some of the committee's recommendations like making GB a "provisional" province and the representation of GB in the national assembly as well as in all constitutional bodies, pending final settlement of the Kashmir 'dispute'.[13] Endorsing these recommendations, the court observed that "the [Sartaj Aziz] Committee itself was acutely aware of the sensitivities of the issue before it and provided its recommendations only after considering their implications, if any, on the status of the Kashmir 'dispute'."[14]

At the same time, the ruling was clearly intended to assert Pakistan's control on Gilgit-Baltistan. Despite declaring GB as a 'disputed' territory, the court nevertheless identified the people of GB as "citizens of Pakistan for all intents and purposes."[15] Even if the SC evoked the Sartaj Aziz committee's suggestions calling for granting greater rights, it still felt short of issuing a directive to the government to ensure these rights to the people of GB. The nature of the ruling substantiates that the SC's intention was only to reinstate the new GB Order and a nominal assurance to people that they deserved speedy justice.

While Pakistan's mainstream media has only highlighted the court's suggestions to grant fundamental rights to locals and treating them on par with Pakistani citizens, it must be realized that the court had raised the same issue two decades earlier. Another change that did not receive much notice is the rise in the number of Pakistani civil servants posted in the region. Compared to the 2018 Order, the quota of Pakistani civil servants posted in GB increased in the top five pay scales listed in the amended Order.

The tables below show the percentage share earmarked for All Pakistan Services officials out of the total number of vacancies in GB.[16,17] (BS 17-21 refers to pay scales of Under Secretary to Additional Secretary ranking officials).

GB Order, 2018

BS-17	BS-18	BS-19	BS-20	BS-21
18%	30%	40%	50%	60%

GB Order, 2018 (amended by Supreme Court)

BS-17	BS-18	BS-19	BS-20	BS-21
25%	40%	50%	60%	65%

This clearly confirms the SC's intention to intensify Pakistan's bureaucratic hold on GB.

The verdict was received with disappointment by the petitioner of the Al-Jehad case, Dr. Ghulam Abbas, who has been raising the issue of GB's marginalization for almost three decades. Abbas was the moving force behind two petitions in the SC in 1999 (Al Jehad Trust case) and 2011 (petition on legal reforms), which also had a key role in prompting the SC to deliver the recent verdict. Expressing dismay, he stated that the people of GB awaited Pakistan's response for the past seven decades but the judiciary too failed to deliver on their expectations.[18] However, the verdict was a reality check for those advocating that GB be incorporated into Pakistan as a fifth province, that any such move would be impossible. At the same time, it still left no stone unturned in tightening Pakistan's control over the region. Abbas demanded that GB be at least given an administrative set-up on the lines of Azad Jammu and Kashmir.

On the one hand, the SC stated that the people of GB could be granted rights on par with Pakistani citizens but on the other, the GB administration is kept under the tight grip of Islamabad. Furthermore, Dr. Abbas highlighted that even the judges of GB's apex court were drawn from among the retired judges in Pakistan on a contractual basis.[19] He considered taking the case to the UN or International Court of Justice, citing that the issue of GB was an international 'dispute'.

Concluding Remarks

Developments in GB since late 2017 only depict Pakistan's inability to grant rights to the people of GB. The then Prime Minister Abbasi's decision to abolish the GB Council during the last days of the PML-N-led government turned out to be merely an eyewash, given the way it was restored by the SC, making the decision a regressive step for the legitimate popular demand to grant greater legislative authority to GB's elected government. Further, the failure to deliver on such basic political freedoms has time and again prompted Islamabad to blame India. Protestors have been dealt with a heavy hand and the government's liberal use of draconian laws like the Anti-Terrorist Act on GB's activists and the state's efforts at terming their agitations as Indian-sponsored have been effective in crushing dissent. In totality, the denial of political rights to the people of GB is something where the army, civilian administration and, in subtle terms, the judiciary happen to be on the same page.

NOTES

1. Jamil Nagri, "Gilgit-Baltistan protesters demand withdrawal of taxes", *Dawn*, Islamabad, November 16, 2017.
2. Ghulam Abbas, "Thousands march towards Gilgit as strike against taxes enters 6th day", *Pakistan Today*, Lahore, December 27, 2017.
3. Jamil Nagri, "PM Decides To Abolish Gilgit-Baltistan Council", *Dawn*, Islamabad, February 17, 2018.
4. Government of Gilgit-Baltisan Order 2018 (Draft), *Pamir Times*.
5. Jamil Nagri, "New law promises more political, judicial powers to Gilgit-Baltistan", *Dawn*, Islamabad, May 22, 2018.
6. Jamil Nagri, 2018. "Appellate Court Suspends GB Order 2018". *Dawn*, Islamabad, June 21, 2018.
7. "SC Restores Gilgit-Baltistan Order 2018", *Daily Times*, Lahore, August 8, 2018.
8. Ibid.
9. Ibid.
10. Read the Government of Gilgit-Baltisan Order 2018 (Draft), *Pamir Times*, Gilgit, May 3, 2018.
11. Supreme Court ruling on Gilgit Baltistan, January 7, 2019, http://www.supremecourt.gov.pk/web/user_files/File/Const.P._50_2018.pdf

12 Supreme Court ruling on Gilgit Baltistan, pages 10-11.
13 Supreme Court ruling, page 19.
14 Afzal Ali Shigri, "GB: The Way Forward", *Dawn*, 2019.
15 Supreme Court ruling on Gilgit Baltistan, January 7, 2019.
16 GB order, 2018, page 61.
17 Supreme Court ruling on Gilgit Baltistan, page 76.
18 GB (Gilgit-Baltistan) Isn't The Part Of Pakistan| Supreme Court's Clear Verdict | Dr. Abbas Petition. 2019. Video. https://www.youtube.com/watch?v=6ktgLBM_RtA&t=107s
19 Ibid.

17

J&K: Developments 2018-19 and Prospects

Lt. Gen. Syed Ata Hasnain

In the early part of mid-2019, J&K is uncharacteristically quiet. The LoC, counter-infiltration grid and the hinterland have seen far lower violence and the streets are less turbulent than any time in the last four years or so. These are cycles which occur in J&K's 30-year-long Pakistan-sponsored and controlled proxy war. There are enough reasons that can be counted for the current phenomenon, among them being the reluctance of Pakistan to run foul with the international community due the acute economic situation it faces. Equally, the risk of an uncontrollable spiral of near-war situations with India is not something very palatable for Pakistan; especially after the decisive knocks it received post-Pulwama. However, to get any measure of the reality of the situation and the prospects of the future, it is necessary to review the events of 2018-19. The primary domains required to be touched include security, political, Pakistan's support, social environment and governance.

It is a truism that violence in J&K occurs in cycles of indeterminate number of years followed by relative calm. After the high violence cycle of 2008-10 there were relatively quieter years in 2011-14 before the build-up began again. The passing of the mantle to the new generation took place with the Burhan Wani movement which gained greater traction in 2015. However, 2016-18 has been characterised by high-violence post the killing of Burhan Wani in July 2016. As casualties of security forces (SF) mounted there was a time in 2016-17 when the ratio of own fatal casualties to the number of terrorists neutralised was almost 1:1, a low never experienced in the past. The strength of terrorists was yet only an estimated 350. A couple of years prior to this, terrorist violence from the Jammu region had receded and come to negligible levels. 2018 began as the second year of Operation All Out, a series of pro-active actions to weed out the terrorist leadership and prevent other terrorists the initiative of a free run. This included a change in tactics for a short duration necessitating large-scale cordon-and-search operations to establish full domination over South Kashmir where the focus had shifted. From the achievement point of view, 2018 was a successful year with neutralisation of 254 terrorists. However, the level of recruitment went up considerably with 190 youth confirmed to have joined the terrorists. In addition, approximately 75 terrorists successfully infiltrated from PoK. Thus, in quantum terms, the terrorist strength eroded in operations was fully made up to 350-plus by the end of 2018.

As has been experienced with the pattern of terrorist activities, there was an effort by the terrorist leadership and the Pakistan deep state to innovate strategy to keep the pressure on the Indian security forces (SF). One of the ways was by targeting families of policemen, isolated policemen on duty, special police officers (SPOs) and Kashmiri soldiers of the Indian Army on leave. This had a social connotation too as large numbers of youth turned up at recruiting rallies of the various SF which worried the separatists and proxy war sponsors. By threatening families and targeting individual soldiers, an act rarely done in the 30-year proxy war, the terrorists displayed a different ruthlessness less witnessed in the J&K region.

In the above period, the Pulwama, Shupiyan, Kulgam and Bijbehara quadrangle has been the main violence-prone zone although Tral and Lidder Valley have also been active. By contrast, North Kashmir has seen lower levels of violence and that too sporadically. Sopore continues to see violence but at much reduced levels. Gandarbal and Bandipur have been relatively stable. However, in J&K, one maxim to be religiously followed is—the absence of violence does not mean normality'. Assessments of the past alluding to returning normality have been belied quite often. Thus, North Kashmir yet carries the potential of revival which could happen with one charismatic terrorist leader and a couple of hard core, radical terrorists infiltrated from PoK through the LoC not too far away. 2018 also witnessed a voluntary halt of operations by the SF for 30 days during Ramzan but the same was unacceptable to the terrorists and their cohorts. The experiment failed and later led to a higher level of violence. The terrorists maintained a dynamic hit-and-run strategy targeting as prominent a personality as Shujaat Bukhari, the editor of the high-profile English newspaper, *Rising Kashmir*. Bukhari had been critical of the Pakistani deep state and the terror groups for not accepting cessation of operations.

The panchayat and municipal elections were held in 2018 with a reduced turnout and boycott by the two mainstream political parties—the National Conference (NC) and the Peoples Democratic Party (PDP). The 'bread and butter' elections as these have come to be called are of little worth unless the necessary legislation is completed for the empowerment of the panchayats which currently remain only on paper. This time around targeting of panchayat officials has not taken place displaying another change in terrorist strategy. The BJP participated in the polls and therefore has some presence at the grassroots level but how far will this translate into any advantage to obtain a few badly needed seats in the J&K Assembly is questionable.

The issue of the Armed Forces Special Powers Act (AFSPA) came to the fore again with the registration of an FIR against Maj. Aditya of 10 Garhwal Rifles for the killing of three civilians after they attempted to lynch some of his men on 27 Jan 2018. AFSPA continues to remain one of the least understood laws in India. Its 1990 version applied to J&K is clearly too weak and provides questionable cover to soldiers functioning in J&K. Branded a draconian law by human rights activists it clearly does not cater for the many contingencies that have come to light with the experience of the last 30 years. If anything, AFSPA needs review, not removal; review for making it more comprehensive to cover contingencies and revision of those sections which give a perception of it being draconian. Very few would realise that AFSPA does not specifically grant any immunity or qualified immunity to a soldier after he retires from service. It is an amendment sorely needed to avoid a midnight knock once a soldier has hung up his boots.

The politics of J&K has been unstable over the last five years. The BJP-PDP coalition, initially considered an ideal working platform to bring the two estranged portions of J&K closer, clearly did not work due to mistrust and tendency to remain segmented into regions. Ideologically different, the two parties clearly had different agendas. It resulted in the breakup of the coalition and imposition of Governor's Rule which continues to this day. It is yet uncertain how well Governor's Rule has worked administratively but in the security domain the continued success of Operation All Out has been facilitated. However, the duration of this arrangement could also have had a salutary effect on the employment of non-security-related aspects pertaining to the hybrid war. The much in demand 'all of government' approach which should have been implemented with vigour does not appear to have manifested itself in full form. This should have included direct outreach, communication and engagement between the people of Jammu and Kashmir regions, de-radicalisation and counter-radicalisation programs, media strategy and an information blitz to counter Pakistan's professional propaganda. Not much is known about the programs that the administration has outlined and is implementing on the ground.

In the social domain, it is apparent that while local recruitment has been considerably diluted, the hold of radical ideology over the youth appears to remain rampant. In the financial domain, the National Investigation Agency's efforts appear to be bearing fruit. The manifestation of success here is usually felt in the quantum of stone-throwing agitations which, in 2019, have taken a lower priority. The further erosion of money in the hands of the separatists is likely to neutralise this capability further.

The most important event of this period was the unfortunate incident of suicide bombing near Pulwama against a CRPF bus which resulted in 40 fatalities. With funerals of martyrs being held in different parts of the country it had a major impact on the collective psyche of the nation. The time being close to the run-up to India's general elections gave the entire episode a political colour. The Jaish-e-Mohammad (JeM) led by Maulana Masood Azhar claimed responsibility for the terrorist act; however, Pakistan refused to bear any responsibility for it despite the clear evidence of the JeM and its leadership existing on its soil. India launched an airstrike with a packet of 12 Mirage aircraft and Israeli beyond-visual-range (BVR) retarder bombs on the JeM training facility at Balakote in Khyber Pakhtunkhwa, killing a large number of under-training terrorists owing allegiance to the JeM. Subsequent actions by Pakistan for a quid pro quo across the LoC left it in a dilemma on the choice of targets since no terror facilities are known to exist in India. The Indian government kept the escalation strictly under control, only communicating its will to surgically strike at terror facilities inside Pakistan. The latter denied the effectiveness of the IAF operation and continued to maintain that Pulwama was a false flag operation by India to obtain a political advantage for the government of the day. Internationally, Pakistan failed to convince the international community although its deft information campaign prevented it being fully in the dock. However, the dynamics of the events in Afghanistan kept Pakistan from being admonished in harsher terms. Pakistan plays an important role in the Afghanistan negotiations between the USA and the Taliban which keeps the US attitude nebulous towards Pakistan's obvious involvement in sponsoring proxy war in J&K. What the Pulwama-Balakote combine has done is to take the escalation to a new level. Another major terrorist act and India will be forced to respond from a higher rung of the ladder with Pakistan attempting to counter the same with its own response. Former senior Pakistani officers claim that this episode has conveyed a clarity that below conventional level Pakistan was fully capable of launching a counter response to anything India chose to do. It considers the nuclear backdrop as sufficient deterrence for any conventional operations by India. The situation is clearly dangerous with Pakistan confident that it can continue to calibrate the situation in J&K and absorb any Indian retribution before responding it its own timeframe. Any Pakistani sponsored terror act in future will be a trigger for a higher escalation which could be in different domains and not necessarily in the military domain alone.

Future Prospects

With the victory of Prime Minister Narendra Modi in the elections, there is a contrasting environment in India and Pakistan. With over 400 billion US$ in forex reserve, India is endeavouring to move on in economic development with the single-minded purpose of sustainable growth of 8-10 per cent. In contrast, Pakistan is in financial doldrums with its strategic autonomy too compromised. It is smitten by China's decision not to support Masood Azhar and the majority of the international community and international financial institutions ranged against it for its inability and virtual refusal to rein in terrorist elements that operate from its soil. The dichotomy lies in the fact that while its civil society too desires peace, the Pakistan Army will not loosen the controls it has over Pakistan's foreign and security policy where targeting India remains one of its primary aims, right from the time of Gen Zia-ul-Haq.

The temporary lull in activities in J&K must be viewed as a tactical ploy by Pakistan until something more sustainable emerges.

The relatively stable situation in J&K must not be misread as an achievement which is what political elements are wont to do. Rather, it should be seen as a window of opportunity to streamline the elusive 'All of Government' approach to simultaneously prevent resurgence of violence, dilute ideas of separatism from the public mind and break the march of religious radicalism which Pakistan's deep state wishes to utilise to create greater linkages with Pan Islamism. This can only happen with direct outreach to the people by representatives of the state and from elsewhere. There is no shortcut to talking with the people, making them realise the advantage of being Indian and not being used as pawns in a proxy war. The political community of J&K itself has to play a crucial role to prevent further estrangement between the Jammu region and the Valley. There needs to be many platforms on which the people of the two regions can interact intellectually, professionally and socially.

The leadership role of the Indian Army in all parts of J&K has been stellar. Fully comprehending the threats of proxy war by virtue of its professional understanding of the spectrum of war, the Army has been the lead organisation along with Intelligence agencies of the Centre and the State. It must continue playing this role and not be misled by notions of transiting situations from public order to law and order, changing patterns of violence or simply absence of violence in some areas of the state. To step back without finally defeating Pakistan's proxy war would be premature. There are yet more cycles of proxy war that Pakistan will test us with.

18

Afghanistan: Different Possibilities for Ensuring Stability

Lt. Gen. Ravi Sawhney

The developments in Afghanistan have strategic implications for the entire South Asian region including India. At present, Afghanistan confronts enormous challenges in achieving political stability, improving security and enhancing economic growth. The decision of the Trump Administration to withdraw troops from Afghanistan as well as the ongoing negotiations with the Taliban has compounded the complexities. The outcomes of the US/NATO withdrawal from the country would have profound implications for the region.

US Withdrawal from Afghanistan

In late-2018, reports emerged regarding President Trump's decision to pull out roughly 7,000 of the estimated 14,000 troops from Afghanistan. It is clear that the growing domestic opposition to the war as well as the high costs of sustaining military operations were key drivers behind the decision. From the point of view of the USA and the West, the case for peace talks with the Taliban, divorced from its mistakes, costs and difficulties, sounds compelling and is also increasingly finding support from Russia and China. Their current narrative talks of 17 years of a US-led war against terrorism in Afghanistan, increase in troop strength in 2017 on one hand, and the enormous cost to Afghanistan, the USA and others in lives and wealth on the other. It also talks of the war having reached a stalemate with an estimated 50 per cent Afghan territory under control of the Taliban as well as the futility of stretching this war indefinitely. Peace talks, therefore, are imperative.

In Afghanistan, the USA embarked on a military campaign in 2001 with the sole objective of 'defeating, disrupting and dismantling' the al-Qaeda which was responsible for the 9/11 attacks. Eighteen years since, while the al-Qaeda has been virtually decimated in Afghanistan-Pakistan, the Taliban remains resilient and is on the ascendancy, both militarily and diplomatically. The insurgency, which has been engaging with multiple international stakeholders over the past years, has become emboldened at the cost of the Afghan government which is the elected and legitimate representative of the Afghan people.

The USA has had six rounds of talks with the Taliban since last September. A hurried peace deal, aimed at achieving peace with the Taliban and bringing it to power at any cost, can potentially cause instability and violence which will be to the detriment of not just Afghanistan but also for the entire region. This process has so far excluded the Afghan government which should have been an important player in any peace process. In other words, the peace talks should be led, owned and controlled by the Ghani government. Any peace deal should promote national reconciliation and preserve the constitutional order, democratic values and basic rights of the people.

Afghan Security Forces

The USA has come a long way in fighting terrorism in Afghanistan and establishing a democratic system. A sudden and rapid exit of forces would lead to the collapse of the constitutional order and the Afghan security forces which have been built through huge investments. A robust security apparatus would act as a bulwark against the rise of terrorism in the country. Afghan security forces will not be able to stem the Taliban tide without operational and financial support from the USA. While it may be true to some extent, the Afghan army is increasingly becoming a well-trained and motivated force which has stood up to the challenge posed by the Taliban, despite suffering a huge number of casualties. Afghanistan, however, does not have the resources to maintain its army. Therefore, the requisite budgetary support needs to be given by the USA and the international community. In the absence of financial support, the Afghan army will not be able to sustain itself and will disintegrate into various militias, posing a danger to the stability of the country/region.

Peace Deal

The peace deal with the Taliban should not be an end goal in itself. What is important is how well the international community, especially the USA can push the Taliban to moderate its ideology in accordance with the Afghan constitution and ensure that the Taliban actually honours its side of the bargain. This, in turn, is likely only when the international community gives its unconditional commitment and support to the Afghan government and people throughout these negotiations and beyond. Any lasting settlement is possible only through gradual and incremental steps and not through a blockbuster deal.

Changes in Afghan Society

Afghan society has changed in the past 17 years and the support for a radical extremist ideology which the Taliban propagates does not find any resonance among the Afghan people. The most likely support for the Taliban ideology can be found only in a few deep conservative rural pockets of the south and the east. The rest of the country follows a much less conservative version of Islam that permits modern technology, elections, sports, music, respect for minorities, women's rights, etc. Therefore, if the Taliban wants to reintegrate into Afghan society, they must respect the aspirations of the people of Afghanistan by moderating their ideology in accordance with the changed realities. Any peace deal with the Taliban must be inclusive in nature and the armed group must reject terrorism and violence, acknowledge people's aspirations, accept women's rights and the Afghan constitution. This constitution, though imperfect in many ways, has stood the test of time. It can definitely be suitably amended but discarding it altogether would be a retrograde step.

Future Engagement with Afghanistan

The most crucial factor which will determine the future of Afghanistan is the level of engagement the international community keeps with the country today as well as in the future. The Afghan people, its fledgling democracy, poor economy and weak security apparatus need a considerable amount of commitment and support including monetary aid and military assistance from the international community. It is important for the international community to understand that the Afghan government and people alone cannot fight the triads of extremism, terrorism, separatism; and transnational organised crimes including drug trafficking which has implications for the region and the world. Therefore, the international community must continue to provide the required funding for governance as well as the security needs of Afghanistan. Especially crucial is the long-term funding of the Afghan security to boost its capability as well as to prevent its disintegration into smaller militias in the absence of funding.

There is a need to bolster Afghanistan's economic growth in order to reduce its dependence on foreign aid. As a landlocked country, Afghanistan requires connectivity in order to break its inaccessibility from the international markets. The US move to exempt Chabahar Port from the sanctions was a very positive move which will contribute to transforming Afghanistan into an independent economy.

Regional Initiatives

The role of regional countries is also important in Afghanistan. A comprehensive regional framework is necessary for durable peace in the country. It is important to involve the regional neighbours in the peace negotiations as stakeholders. Any attempt to keep the regional players out will breed suspicion. The existing multilateral regional initiatives on Afghanistan which includes the Heart of Asia process, International Contact Group on Afghanistan, Quadrilateral Coordination Group, Moscow Format Consultations, and SCO-Afghanistan Contact Group have not been able to make any decisive and real impact. The reason for the inadequate progress of these initiatives is the competing tendency of various countries in the region to gain maximum influence in Afghanistan. Therefore, none of these regional initiatives have the required competence and vision to solve the Afghan crisis. The composition of the regional mechanism is important. It should neither be too limited such as the Kabul process or Quadrilateral Coordination Group nor should it be too large such as the International Contact Group which would be functionally unviable. The USA could take the lead in forming such a group.

Additional Points for Consideration while Negotiating Peace Deal

While negotiating a peace deal with the Taliban, a few other important aspects that are required to be kept in view are:

(a) The USA should be careful not to leave Afghanistan and the region worse off than it is at the moment. The present time table is too rushed for a stable outcome.

(b) While the USA will withdraw, no corresponding check on Pakistan's interference is visible that has the potential to upset the military and negotiating balance.

(c) Interim government will create a dangerous constitutional vacuum that cannot be filled by power-sharing between jihadi leaders and the Taliban. That may result in the 1990s situation that created al-Qaeda.

(d) Present Taliban intransigence could be an opportunity to create intra-Afghan consensus in order to build a common front against the Taliban at the negotiating table.

(e) The USA should support timely elections to avoid a power vacuum and chaos. President Trump, we are certain, would like to leave a long-lasting and not short-term legacy.

Conclusion

A peace deal before elections as ex-President Karzai has called for is unrealistic. The EU's call for peace and elections is somewhat disingenuous. While it may be impossible to delink the two, Taliban intransigence on participation of the Afghan government in peace talks can be used to take a pause in the negotiations and use the elections as a forum for presidential aspirants to bring their vision of peace to the people of Afghanistan. This could then become a basis of a common negotiating position.

19

Afghanistan-Pakistan Relations: Frosty Neighbours?

Yatharth Kachiar

Introduction

The geographical proximity, linguistic, ethnic, cultural and religious affinity and strong historical connection have woven the destinies of Afghanistan and Pakistan for long. However, despite these commonalities, the relations between these two countries have always been less than amenable. Historically, the relations between the two countries have been marred by border disputes, proxy wars and political disagreements. The contentious nature of relations between Afghanistan and Pakistan is mainly because of the narrow security conception adopted by the Pakistani state towards its neighbours. The zero-sum approach adopted by Pakistan towards India, led the governing elites in Pakistan to search for 'strategic depth' on its western border in Afghanistan. For the ruling elites in Rawalpindi, the policy of achieving strategic depth in Afghanistan meant establishing a state on its western border which is politically and militarily dependent on Pakistan.

Recently, the relations between the two countries have seen a downward trend largely because of Pakistan's consistent support to the Taliban and its interference in the internal affairs of Afghanistan. In January 2019, President Ashraf Ghani criticized Pakistan's policy of providing safe haven to the terrorists in Afghanistan when he said, "key to peace was in Afghanistan but keys to war are in Islamabad, Quetta, and Rawalpindi."[1] Further, President Trump's decision to withdraw the US security forces from Afghanistan as early as possible has enhanced the unease in the dynamics between Pakistan and Afghanistan. In the previous decade, Pakistan had shared a troubled relationship with the USA because of its unrelenting support to the Afghan Taliban and the Haqqani Network. The USA has accused these groups of carrying out deadly attacks against the Afghan army and US security forces in Afghanistan. However, President Trump's decision to negotiate a settlement with the Taliban has once again made Pakistan an important element in the US strategic designs. This article attempts to analyze the ongoing trend in the relations between Pakistan and Afghanistan against the backdrop of a rapidly-changing geopolitical situation.

Political Relations

Afghanistan-Pakistan Action Plan for Peace and Solidarity (APAPPS)

As noted earlier, the relations between Afghanistan and Pakistan are tarnished with years of hostility and mistrust. In order to end this mutual suspicion of each other's motives and to further enhance peace and cooperation, the two countries signed the Afghanistan-Pakistan Action Plan for Peace and Solidarity (APAPPS) in 2018. It is a bilateral framework based on seven principles including Pakistan's support to Afghan-owned and Afghan-led peace process, denying their respective territories for anti-state activities against the other country and a commitment to avoid territorial and aerial violations.[2]

Under APAPPS, the two nations established six working groups, namely, Politico-diplomatic, military-to-military, Intelligence-to-Intelligence, Economy and Trade, Refugees and a review committee to boost necessary cooperation in the areas of mutual interest. However, apart from the inaugural meeting of the working groups that took place in July 2018, the plan has not been able to achieve the desired results largely due to poor enforcement. In fact, in September 2018, President Ghani urged the visiting Foreign Minister of Pakistan to fully implement the APAPPS.[3]

Refugee Issue

One of the biggest irritants between Afghanistan and Pakistan has been the presence of a large number of Afghan refugees in Pakistan. According to official data, Pakistan is home to a total estimated population of 3 million Afghan refugees out of which 1.4 million are registered as refugees. Most of these were born in Pakistan and belong to the second and third-generation of refugees who have never been to their country of origin. Despite being born in Pakistan, they are still not considered Pakistani citizens.

The trilateral agreement signed between Pakistan, Afghanistan and the UN makes Pakistan obligated to issue Proof of Registration (PoR) cards to the Afghan refugees who have registered themselves with the UNHCR. These cards "protect against risks such as extortion, arbitrary arrest and detention as well as deportation under Pakistan's Foreigner's Act."[4] However, the friction in relations between Afghanistan and Pakistan has direct repercussions on the status of Afghan refugees in Pakistan. Many times, Pakistani authorities have denied renewing the PoR cards for refugees thus threatening their stay in the country. In early 2018, the decision of the Pakistani authorities not to extend the Proof of Registration cards (PoR) to the Afghan refugees again created a crisis situation. The denial of a PoR card meant that they could be forcefully deported to their country of origin whenever the authorities demand. However, the issue was resolved after a series of protests by civil society activists and the deadline was finally extended for another 60 days.[5] The current validity of PoR cards is till 30 June 2019 after which the Afghan refugees will once again be at the mercy of the Pakistani authorities for continuing their legal stay in Pakistan.[6]

Interestingly, under Section 4 of the Pakistani Citizenship Act of 1951, any person born on Pakistani soil after the enactment of this act is entitled to Pakistani citizenship. However, this 'citizenship by birth' is continuously denied to Afghan refugees.[7,8] As a scholar observes, "instead of the dark green Pakistani passports and national identity cards that citizens get, they're assigned only Proof of Registration (PoR) cards, which entitle them to freedom of movement and temporary legal status in the country. Islamabad bars them from purchasing property, vehicles, and even SIM cards."[9] Further, refugee children are not allowed to enrol in public schools or universities. Pregnant Afghan mothers are frequently denied medical care by hospitals on the pretext that they cannot issue birth certificates to the infants.[10]

After coming to power, Prime Minister Imran Khan sparked a debate in the country by suggesting that he will grant citizenship to the children of Afghan refugees born in Pakistan.[11] However, this received a serious backlash from the opposition parties which forced the Prime Minister to retract from his previous statement.[12,13] Afghan refugees received some relief when, in February 2019, Prime Minister Imran Khan permitted registered Afghan refugees to open bank accounts in order to include them in the formal economy of the country.[14] Overall, the refugee issue between the two countries is not going to die down any time soon. The problems of arbitrary arrests, harassment and fear of deportation will continue to haunt the Afghan refugees for a long time to come.

Pashtun Issue: FATA Merger and Pashtun Tahafuz Movement

The most intricate factor in Pakistan-Afghanistan relations is the issue of the Durand Line. Afghanistan rejected the Durand Line on the grounds that the Treaty of Gandamak (1879) and the Durand agreement (1893) were unjust treaties imposed by the British. Pakistani state elites already perceive the presence of India on its eastern border through a narrow security lens. In this scenario, the disputed western border enhances the threat perception of the ruling elites in Pakistan. Further, what heightens Pakistan's insecurity is the fact that both sides of the Durand Line are inhabited by common Pashtun population with similar customs, traditions, language, religion and ethnicity. This makes the Pakistani territory vulnerable towards any separatist movement on its western border. The Pashtuns living on both sides of the Durand Line have never accepted the arbitrary demarcation of the boundary between Pakistan and Afghanistan.

The issue came to the forefront once again when, in 2018, Pakistan merged the Federally Administered Tribal Areas (FATA) with Khyber Pakhtunkhwa (KPK) province. The decision received a serious backlash from the Ghani government who called it the "contravention of 1921 treaty signed between Afghanistan and the then British India."[15] On the other hand, Pakistan warned Afghanistan to refrain from interfering in its internal affairs. The Pakistani government defended the FATA merger by stating that it reflected the will of the people of Pakistan.[16] However, some of the tribal elders from the FATA region and some religious parties opposed Pakistan's decision to merge FATA with KPK.[17]

The FATA area comprised seven agencies and six frontier regions and shared its western border with Afghanistan. The bill was approved by the Pakistan parliament by 229 votes in favour and one against. The hardline parties such as the Jamiat-e-Ulema-Islam–Fazlur (JUI-F) and Pashtunkhwa Milli Awami Party (PMAP) opposed the move of merging FATA with KP province.[18] Previously, the region was ruled by Pakistan on the basis of colonial-era laws called Frontier Crimes Regulations (FCR). It gave the local leaders and tribal heads more autonomy over the decision-making of the region. For a very long time, the region was not even accommodated in the political process of the country. Pakistan's constitution granted the right to vote to all its citizens after independence; however, FATA's residents received it only in 1997. Moreover, the Political Party Act of Pakistan was not applicable to the region thereby prohibiting the residents of the region to form political parties and contest in the general elections.[19] As a scholar observes, "it is one of Pakistan's poorest regions with more than 60 per cent of the 3 million people living below the poverty line and there is no state-run education or healthcare system."[20]

The Pakistani establishment's decision to change the status quo of the region can be attributed to two major reasons. Firstly, the counter-terrorism operations undertaken by the Pakistan military in recent times can be successful in the long term only when the FATA region is integrated politically, economically and socially into the mainstream Pakistani society. The region is notorious for being a hotbed of extremism and radicalism. Secondly, in order to cement the internal security of the Pakistani state, it was imperative from the point of view of the Pakistani military to integrate the FATA region well within the internal security structure of the country. The merger will make it far easier for the Pakistani state to implement the "comprehensive border management structure" on its border with Afghanistan which is the main entry point of anti-state elements into Pakistan.[21]

In addition to the merger of the FATA with KP province, the issue of the Pashtun Tahafuz Movement (PTM) in Pakistan has seriously impacted the relations between Pakistan and Afghanistan. The movement began against the extra-judicial killing of a young model Naqeebullah Mehsud in Karachi in January 2018 by the military. The protests against the killing and the state suppression quickly spread to various parts of the country and received huge international attention as well. The demands put forward by the PTM include "removal of arbitrary check posts and landmines that are scattered across the tribal belt, a return of "missing people" and setting up of a judicial inquiry to find those who have been picked up by the Pakistan military over the years and an end to the military subjugation of their home."[22] However, instead of addressing the demands of its own grieving population, Pakistan has blamed India and Afghanistan for stirring the Pashtun population of the country by providing financial aid to the PTM movement.[23]

In February 2019, tensions between the two countries were fuelled after the crackdown and arrest of PTM protestors in a rally in Islamabad. Reacting harshly to the crackdown, President Ashraf Ghani tweeted, "the Afghan government has serious concerns about the violence perpetrated against peaceful protesters and civil activists in Khyber Pakhtunkhwa and Balochistan."[24] Earlier, in February 2018 President Ghani conveyed his support for the Pashtun Long March when he tweeted that the main purpose of the march "is to mobilize citizens against fundamentalism and terrorism in the region."[25] Pakistan rejected these claims by the Ghani government and termed it as "gross interference" in its internal affairs.[26]

Security-related Issues

Border Fencing

Another unilateral decision of Pakistan to build a border fence on its western border with landlocked Afghanistan has become a source of tension between the two countries. In addition to the border fence, Pakistan will also build new forts and posts along the western border and increase the strength of troops on its western border for effective patrolling.[27] The plan to build a 2,600-km-long fence along the border with Afghanistan is aimed at preventing the infiltration of anti-state elements across the border. However, Kabul rejects any border security plan by Islamabad because of the disputed status of the Durand Line itself. On Pakistan's declaration of fencing the border in 2006, President Karzai had said that the fencing will not achieve any other purpose but it will surely divide the same families living on both sides of the border.[28] The issue of border fencing was further raised by the Afghan government at the UN when in 2007 the Karzai government wrote a letter to UN Secretary General Ban ki-Moon and conveyed its distress over the fencing of the border. As a scholar noted, "Karzai's views were also supported by the nationalists from Pashtunkhwa and Balochistan provinces of Pakistan, who termed the decision to fence the border as detrimental to the social and economic interests of the ethnic Pashtun tribes. It was also opposed by the Muttahida Majlis Amal, a group of religious parties who were then in government both in Pashtunkhwa and Balochistan. The tribesmen gathered on the Afghanistan side and demanded that the government prevent the fencing."[29]

In January 2019, the Pakistan army stated that the work on 900 km of the fence along the Afghanistan-Pakistan border had been completed. In October 2018, the fencing of the border led to an exchange of fire between Pakistani and Afghan forces near the border town of Chaman.[30] In further retaliation, the Pakistani border authorities "closed the Friendship Gate near Chaman which left thousands of people stranded on both sides of the Pak-Afghan border."[31] Further, the residents on the Afghanistan side of the border also expressed their angst over Pakistan's policy of building the fence and thus dividing the families living on both sides of the border. In April 2018, the residents of Khost province clashed with the Pakistani military personnel in Zazi Maidan district.[32] Pakistan has violated ceasefire norms on the border innumerable times in the past few years. In February 2019, the Ghani government lodged a formal complaint in the UN against "violation of its territory by Pakistan military, including the shelling of Afghan territory, violation of its airspace by military aircraft and construction of military posts and barriers on its soil."[33] In its complaint, Afghanistan mentioned that since January 2018, "Pakistani troops were involved in 161 violations and fired more than 6000 mortar and artillery shells into Afghan territory."[34] The complaint also accused Pakistani-based elements of the assassination of the police chief of Kandahar, General Abdul Raziq Achekzai, who took some strong measures to prevent the installation of border fencing by Pakistan in his province.[35] Despite the protests by Afghanistan, the work on border fencing continued without any hindrance. In fact, in May 2019, Pakistan inaugurated the work on border fencing in Balochistan which includes the building of forts and watchtowers every 3 km of the border to ensure proper monitoring.[36]

Peace Talks

After years of a rift with the USA over the issue of supporting terrorist groups, Pakistan again resumed the centre-stage in America's foreign policy against the background of President Trump's decision to withdraw US security forces from Afghanistan. In December 2018, President Trump wrote a letter to Pakistan Prime Minister Imran Khan seeking Islamabad's "assistance and facilitation in achieving a negotiated settlement of the Afghan war."[37] Pakistan's hold over the Taliban ensures that it remains an important player in any final outcome in Afghanistan. It is crucial to understand the relentlessness of the disruptive role played by the state of Pakistan in Afghanistan. As a scholar observes, "while there are multiple factors that have caused the current war in Afghanistan to persist for nearly two decades—including the failure of governance and corruption, Taliban's access to resources from foreign donors and the drug trade—a sanctuary in Pakistan has been critical."[38] Pakistan has given financial and logistics support to the Taliban and the Haqqani Network and has provided medical care for Taliban fighters.[39] The Pakistani establishment provided a free hand to the Taliban to establish a sanctuary on its soil with the freedom to operate in Pakistan.[40]

A continuing failure to curb Pakistan's leadership from supporting terrorist groups in the future will eventually lead to the failure of any peace deal in Afghanistan. The incessant support provided by Pakistan to the Taliban and the Haqqani Network has undermined the ability of the international community, especially Washington, to achieve even limited goals in Afghanistan on its own including the peace deal. Any future deal with the Taliban will not be sustainable unless the state of Pakistan relinquishes its policy of supporting state-sponsored terrorism. It is important for the international community to pressurize Pakistan in a way that it becomes part of a solution in Afghanistan rather than a problem. President Ghani reiterated the same sentiments in Davos in January 2018 when he said, "Our fundamental problem with Pakistan is their inaction in removing the shadow of violence."[41]

Further, Afghanistan lodged a formal complaint in the UN Security Council against the role played by Pakistan in the peace process. In a strongly-worded letter, Afghanistan criticized the Pakistan government's move to invite the Taliban delegation to meet Prime Minister Imran Khan in February 2019. The Afghan government regretted the policy pursued by Pakistan and conveyed that "it amounts to official recognition and legitimization of an armed group that poses a serious threat to security and stability of Afghanistan."[42] The tensions between the two nations increased further when in March 2019 Imran Khan stated that "the Kabul government was a hurdle in the peace process."[43] He even suggested that Afghanistan should form an interim government. The remarks received serious backlash from the Ghani government who considered it as gross meddling in the internal affairs of Afghanistan and in protest recalled its ambassador from Islamabad.[44]

Economic Relations

As a landlocked country, trade and development in Afghanistan are hindered by the country's lack of access to the sea as well as its inaccessibility from the international markets. This obstacle imposed by the geographical location is further compounded by the uncompromising attitude of Pakistan as a transit state. Despite repeated requests from both India and Afghanistan, Pakistan has constantly denied a transit trade route to India for the export of its goods to Afghanistan. In fact, Pakistan has repeatedly blocked Afghanistan's trade with India through the Wagah border despite having agreed to the now-lapsed Afghanistan-Pakistan Transit Trade Agreement (APTTA).

To overcome the obstacles imposed by the geography and negative mindset of the Pakistani establishment, the Government of Afghanistan has been working closely with countries such as India to establish alternative routes of connectivity. One such initiative was the establishment of an air freight corridor connecting New Delhi and Mumbai with Kabul in 2017. Its aim is to encourage bilateral trade between the two countries, enhance the regional connectivity of Afghanistan by giving it direct access to the Indian market, allow Afghan businessmen and farmers to benefit from India's economic growth and trade networks and to export their perishable goods to Indian markets without any hindrance.[45]

The consistent denial of a transit route to India by the Pakistani establishment is part of its years-old zero-sum approach vis-à-vis India especially in relation to Afghanistan. In its bid to achieve so-called 'strategic depth' in Afghanistan in relation to India, the Pakistani establishment has always preferred a state on its western borders which is economically and militarily dependent on Pakistan. In order to accomplish its objectives, Pakistan has repeatedly resorted to economic strangulation of Afghanistan by denying it the transit trade route. According to estimates of the Ministry of Commerce and Industry, the closing of the Durand Line for 30 days in 2017 by Pakistan resulted in the loss of US$ 100 million for Afghanistan.[46]

Till recently, Afghanistan's main access to global and regional markets was the port of Karachi. That is why Pakistan's ability to close its borders or restrict the transport of goods puts Afghanistan in an extremely vulnerable position. However, the opening of the Iranian port of Chabahar in December 2017 has provided Afghanistan with alternative routes for trade and commerce and has considerably reduced its dependency on Pakistan.[47] Moreover, to further curtail its reliance on Pakistan and to overcome the geographical barriers, the Afghanistan Government has pushed for an aggressive air corridor program to boost its trade and development. In addition to the India-Afghanistan air freight corridor which was opened in 2017, the recent opening of air routes from Afghanistan to Turkey, Europe, Russia, China and the UAE will further improve the connectivity of the country to the global markets.[48,49] According to statistics provided by the SIGAR Report, Afghanistan's exports via air corridor have grown by 70 per cent from USD 230 million in 2015 to USD 391 million in 2017.[50]

On the other hand, Pakistan's trade with Afghanistan has dwindled in recent times. According to the latest figures released by the State Bank of

Pakistan, exports to Afghanistan had dropped by 17.68 per cent from USD 739.233 million in July-December in 2017 to USD 608.533 million in the same period in 2018.[51] Moreover, the figures released by the Afghanistan Chamber of Commerce and Industry show that in recent times, Iran has overtaken Pakistan as Afghanistan's biggest trade partner. The trade between Iran and Afghanistan from March 2017 to March 2018 stood at USD 1.98 billion, whereas, trade between Afghanistan-Pakistan during the same period was USD 1.2 billion.[52]

The opening of new avenues of global connectivity for Afghanistan has led to the decline of Pakistan's hold over the Afghan economy. The Chief Executive Officer of Afghanistan, Dr. Abdullah Abdullah, at the World Economic Forum Summit, 2019, in Davos, stated, "we must free the rationale of strong trade and economic ties from the clutches of narrowly defined security-centric conceptions in our relations. Countries should not have to bulk-trade through air corridors or circuitous routes when there are cheaper alternatives."[53] The false and narrow conception of security adopted by Pakistan has become a hindrance in Pakistan-Afghanistan relations. At the same time, it thwarts the efforts of Afghan people towards a better and prosperous future.

Conclusion

Pakistan's policy of seeing Afghanistan through a narrow security prism has proved to be the biggest hindrance towards any positive development in the relations between these two countries. This is precisely the reason why any action plan towards peace and solidarity such as APAPPS has not produced any viable results. The withdrawal of US security forces from Afghanistan will endanger the nascent Afghan democracy and state institutions. Moreover, the increase in the attacks by the Taliban despite the ongoing peace process casts a shadow of doubt about the real intention of the armed group. It is highly likely that rather than peace, the Taliban forces are seeking full power in Kabul. This is precisely the reason behind their consistent denial to accept the Afghan constitution or initiate a dialogue with the democratically elected Afghan government. The moral, financial and ideological support provided by Pakistan to the Taliban risks the legitimacy of the Ghani government and threatens the very existence of Afghanistan itself. Any final solution to the Afghan problem must protect the hope and aspirations of its people, as well as the fragile ethnic fabric of the country. In order to achieve this, it is imperative that Pakistan relinquish its support to the Taliban and the Haqqani Network. Moreover, any hasty effort to end the war might lead to more bloodshed with the possibility of civil war and will have far-reaching consequences for the stability in Afghanistan, Pakistan and the whole region. The key to better Afghanistan-Pakistan relations also lies in the Pakistan establishment's ability to forgo its securitized approach towards Afghanistan. As a scholar observed, "it is only when the army accepts Afghanistan as a sovereign country entitled to have its own policies that best serve its own interests and realizes that the Afghans are first and foremost Afghans, that a dent will be made in Pak-Afghan relations."[54]

NOTES

1. "Pakistan holds 'keys to war', says Afghan president", *Dawn*, Islamabad, January 31, 2019.
2. "Afghanistan-Pakistan Action Plan for Peace and Solidarity", at https://afghanstudiescenter.org/2018/05/16/what-is-afghanistan-pakistan-action-plan-for-peace-and-solidarity-apapps/.
3. "Afghan President emphasizes need to implement APAPPS to Pakistan FM", *Arab News*, Jeddah, September 15, 2018.
4. "Pakistan begins to issue new cards to Afghan refugees, UN confirms", UNHCR, at https://www.refworld.org/docid/53108dbe4.html
5. "Pakistan Gives Afghan Refugees Another 60 Days", *Tolo News,* Kabul, February 1, 2018.
6. "Government extends validity of PoR cards until 30 June", UNHCR, athttps://unhcrpk.org/wp-content/uploads/2018/11/Government-extends-validity-of-PoR-cards-until-30-June-2019.pdf.
7. Pakistan Citizenship Act of 1951, URL: https://www.refworld.org/pdfid/3ae6b4ffa.pdf
8. Zuha Siddiqui, "For Afghan refugees, Pakistan is a nightmare—but also Home", *Foreign Policy*, May 9, 2019.
9. Ibid.
10. Ibid.
11. "Pakistan PM Khan vows to grant Afghan refugees citizenship, CNN, Atlanta, September 18, 2018.
12. "PPP leader lashes out at PM over plans to grant Pakistani citizenship to refugees", *The Express Tribune*, Karachi, September 18, 2018.
13. "Pakistan's Imran Khan skirts issue of Afghan refugees' citizenship", *The Guardian*, London, September 18, 2018.
14. "Imran Khan allows registered Afghan refugees to open bank accounts in Pakistan", *The Economic Times*, Mumbai, February 25, 2019.
15. Masooud Ansar, "Afghanistan Criticizes Pakistan's Unilateral Decision Over FATA", *Tolo News*, Kabul, May 27, 2018.
16. Tahir Khan, Afghanistan objects to KP-FATA merger, *Daily Times*, Lahore, May 27, 2018.
17. "Tribal Elders Oppose FATA, Khyber Pakhtunkhwa Merge", *Tolo News*, Kabul, May 29, 2018.
18. Ibid.
19. Umair Jamal, "What the FATA merger means for Pakistan", *South Asian Voices*, Washington DC, June 6, 2018.
20. Ibid.

21 Ibid.
22 Kriti M Shah, "Pakistan military can't handle growing Pashtun storm, so it's blaming countries like India", May 3 2019, ORF, at https://www.orfonline.org/research/pakistan-military-cant-handle-growing-pashtun-storm-so-its-blaming-countries-like-india-50473/
23 "'Time is up': DG ISPR warns PTM leadership in press conference", *Dawn*, Islamabad, April 29, 2019.
24 Saad Sayeed, "Pakistan activists' arrests fuel tension with Afghanistan", Reuters, London, February 7, 2019.
25 See Link https://twitter.com/ashrafghani/status/961898662866620416?lang=en
26 Saad Sayeed, "Pakistan activists' arrests fuel tension with Afghanistan", Reuters, London, 7 February 7, 2019.
27 "COAS briefed on border fencing, development progress in North Waziristan: ISPR", *Dawn*, Islamabad, May 18, 2019.
28 "Afghan Angry at Pakistan's Plan for Mines and Fence on Border", *The New York Times*, New York, December 29, 2006.
29 Sayed Wiqar Ali Shah, "Fencing of the Durand Line and its impact", *Internationales AsienForum*, 44 (1–2), p. 99.
30 "Pakistani, Afghan forces exchange fire near Chaman", *Dawn*, Islamabad, October 15, 2018.
31 Ibid.
32 "Troops Arrive In Khost As Clash With Pakistani Army Continues", *Tolo News*, Kabul, April 15, 2018.
33 "Afghanistan moves UN over violations by Pak military on its soil", *Hindustan Times*, New Delhi, February 25, 2019.
34 Ibid.
35 Ibid.
36 "Bajwa inaugurates fencing of Pak-Afghan border in Balochistan", *Dawn*, Islamabad, May 9, 2018.
37 "Letter to PM: Trump 'acknowledges Afghan war cost both USA, Pakistan'," *Dawn*, December 3, 2018.
38 Seth G. Jones, "The insurgent Sanctuary in Pakistan", CSIS Brief, Washington DC, September 11, 2018.
39 "Ghani Accuses Pakistan of Treating Wounded Taliban Fighters", VOA News, Washington DC, August 17, 2018.
40 Seth G Jones, "The Insurgent Sanctuary in Pakistan", CSIS Brief, Washington DC, September 11, 2018.
41 "Ghani Says Problem With Pakistan Is Their Inaction", *Tolo News*, January 24, 2019.
42 "Afghanistan protest to UN on Pakistan's role in Taliban Peace Talks", *The Economic Times*, Mumbai, February 17, 2019.
43 "Pakistan PM's remarks on Afghan peace process stir diplomatic row", Al Jazeera, Doha, March 29, 2019.
44 Afghanistan recalls ambassador in row over Pakistan PM remarks, Reuters, London, March 26, 2019.
45 "India and Afghanistan establish Direct Air Freight Corridor", at https://mea.gov.in/press-releases.htm?dtl/28546/India_and_Afghanistan_establish_Direct_Air_Freight_Corridor.

46 Zabihullah Jahanmal, "Torkham Closure 'Damaged' Pakistan's Reputation", *Tolo News*, Kabul, March 21, 2017.
47 Private Sector Development and Economic Growth: Lessons from the U.S. experience in Afghanistan", SIGAR Report, p. 18.
48 "Air cargo route opens from northern Afghanistan to Turkey, Europe", Reuters, London, January 9, 2019.
49 "Afghanistan opens air cargo corridors with Europe, Russia, China, and UAE", Afghanistan Chambers of Commerce and Industry, Kabul, September 27, 2018.
50 SIGAR Quarterly Report, October 2018, at https://www.sigar.mil/pdf/quarterlyreports/2018-10-30qr-section3-economic.pdf, p. 138.
51 "Pakistan's Export of Goods to Afghanistan Dwindles", *Tolo News*, Kabul, January 23, 2019.
52 F.M. Shakil, "Steep fall in Pakistan-Afghanistan bilateral trade", *Asia Times*, Hong Kong, October 10, 2018.
53 Mir Aqa, "Political Rivalry A Barrier To Economic Growth In S. Asia: CEO", *Tolo News*, Kabul, January 23, 2019.
54 Tilak Devasher (2016), *Pakistan: Courting the Abyss*, Harper Collins, Noida, p. 322.

20

Allah, Army and America in Pakistan's National Life

G. Parthasarthy

Pakistanis with a sense of humour have maintained for decades that their lives are determined by the three indispensable "A's": "Allah, Army and America." They aver that while "Allah" the Almighty is benevolent, the "Army" rules them ruthlessly and "America" dominates their national life. Jokes about the "get rich quick" approach of the military brass in Pakistan are now commonplace. They arise from the military's entry into vast areas of industry, commerce, banking and most importantly, real estate. Senior army officials acquire huge properties by virtually free allotment of large areas of urban and agricultural land. But despite the fact that the Pakistan army was responsible for the disintegration of the country in 1971, and for Pakistan's descent into virtual economic bankruptcy, the military brass still proclaims that it is the guardian of Pakistan's "ideological and geographical frontiers."

Its transgressions and culpability notwithstanding, the army remains Pakistan's "holy cow." It uses coercion to ensure that it cannot be criticized by the media, politicians or even the judiciary. It is the hegemony of its military that has led Pakistan to virtual bankruptcy. Pakistan is now faced with a situation where it lags behind Bangladesh whose people it once held in contempt in virtually every economic indicator. It is Pakistan's elected politicians and people who pay the price for the army's national ambitions and its insatiable appetite for absolute power without any legal or constitutional responsibility. No one should, therefore, be surprised when India continues to be held responsible by the Pakistan's army and elite for all the country's problems and woes.

In recent days, there is one country, other than India, which is held responsible in Pakistan for the country's growing tales of woe. This is the United States of America. The routine discourse nowadays in Pakistan is to claim that the "unreliable" Americans are hand in glove with a "wily India," to let down and disappoint an "old ally." What is ignored and forgotten by many Pakistanis, while slamming the Americans, is that Pakistan has developed a reputation of being duplicitous practitioner in its "War on Terror." These less than positive sentiments about Pakistan prevail across a very wide cross-section of public opinion in the USA, especially in both houses of the US Congress.

Most Americans have lost faith and trust in Pakistan because Pakistan can no longer credibly deny that it has provided safety, safe havens, weapons and logistical support to the Taliban and an assortment of radical, armed, Islamist outfits. Around 2,400 American soldiers have lost their lives in Afghanistan, thanks to Pakistani duplicity. Pakistan got an estimated $ 25 billion of American economic and military assistance while arming, training and providing safe haven to the Taliban and hosting the mastermind of 9/11, Osama bin Laden, in the cantonment city of Abbotabad, located virtually on the doorstep of the Pakistan Military Academy. The person who arranged Osama bin Laden's stay in Abbotabad, Brigadier Ejaz Shah, is now Pakistan's Interior Minister, in the Imran Khan Government. As the saying goes: "The more things change, the more they are the same'!!

But things have changed vastly in recent years in the US-Pakistani relationship. President Donald Trump has made no secret of his dislike for and his distrust of Pakistan. American economic assistance to Pakistan has ceased. Pakistan is going through a serious economic crisis with its foreign exchange reserves hovering round $ 10 billion. Saudi Arabian and UAE assistance has been promised but will depend heavily on American approval. What these two cash-rich Arab States have provided in foreign exchange has been measured and small. Cash flows from them to Pakistan will depend largely on American approvals. China provides resources for projects on the China-Pakistan Economic Corridor. But it provides precious little by way of concessional foreign exchange flows to address Pakistan's continuing Balance of Payments crisis.

It is now clear that it is going to be very difficult, if not impossible, for Pakistan to address its foreign exchange crisis without IMF support, which will be forthcoming only if the USA approves. The Trump Administration has acted very differently from its predecessors, who blindly took Pakistani assertions of good intentions at face value and loosened their purse strings. The USA is now making a number of demands for clearing IMF assistance to Pakistan, including asking for detailed information on Chinese projects under the CPEC and Chinese assistance for defence projects like production of JF-17 fighters and supply of submarines and frigates to Pakistan. While President Trump recognises that he needs Pakistani assistance to get a face-saving withdrawal of American forces from Afghanistan, he would find it difficult to achieve his aim as long as the Taliban, which is now sensing victory, refuses to deal realistically with the Afghan Government, despite American Special Envoy Zalmay Khalilzad's exertions.

Adding to Pakistan's problems in dealing with the Trump Administration, whose members distrust it intensely, is the fact that there is little support for Islamabad and Rawalpindi in both Houses of the US Congress. India needs to bear these developments closely in mind in crafting and dealing with its diplomacy in the entire "Afpak" region. Pakistan has brought China and Russia into the picture to get the USA to moderate its position on Afghanistan. The Taliban recognises that Moscow and Beijing are not averse to promoting its ambitions. Given its brutal mistreatment of Muslims in Xinjiang, China would not like to earn Taliban wrath, distrust or hostility in the current domestic situation.

The distrust between the Taliban and large sections of the Afghan public, particularly in the non-Pashtun areas of Afghanistan, is deep. With presidential elections in Afghanistan due later this year, India would be required to keep in touch with a wide cross-section of the Afghan political leadership, to ensure that policy makers in Afghanistan remain on the same page with it in the coming months. This is of crucial importance, while working with the USA and others to ensure that Pakistan does not succeed in its ambitions of making Afghanistan's territory an integral part of its quest for "strategic depth," enabling it to promote terrorism and religious extremism across its entire neighbourhood.

21

Pakistan, Iran and Saudi Arabia

Amb. Dinkar P. Srivastava

Iran under Shah became Pakistan's largest bilateral donor between 1974 and 1976. The equation changed after the revolution and Soviet invasion of Afghanistan. Pakistan started receiving large amounts of aid from Saudi Arabia, which agreed to match dollar for dollar aid given to the Mujahideen by the Americans. The foreign-funded jehad in Afghanistan had a domestic corollary in Pakistan, which saw greater Islamisation under the Zia regime. This also saw the rise of Shia-Sunni tensions in the country. Iran and Pakistan compete for influence in Afghanistan. With Saudi Arabia, Pakistan has at best a client relationship. Pakistan's former Army Chief General Raheel Sharif was chosen by Saudi Arabia to head the Islamic NATO, whose chief aim is to contain Iran. Pakistan has been very successful in receiving assistance from both Iran and Saudi Arabia without necessarily contributing to the security of either. But this policy is subject to the law of diminishing returns, as shown by the Iranian reaction to recent terror attacks in Sistan-Balochistan on IRGC personnel by elements based in Pakistan. The IRGC chief publically cautioned Pakistani people not to allow Saudi money to influence their country.

2018 saw political transition in Pakistan at a time of deepening of economic crisis. Saudi Arabia went through a phase of Western criticism and isolation over the Khashoggi murder. Iran came under renewed US sanctions after President Trump withdrew the USA from the nuclear deal on May 8. The sectarian rift continued to affect Saudi-Iranian relations. The US decision to draw down forces from Syria as well as Afghanistan increased uncertainties. Against this background, Saudi Crown Prince Mohammad Bin Salman visited Pakistan on 17-18 February.

Three days before the visit of the Saudi Crown Prince to Pakistan, a terror attack in Sistan-Balochistan province of Iran on 14 February killed 27 members of Iran's Revolutionary Guards Corps (IRGC). Iran blamed groups based in Pakistan and promised retribution. Pakistan's promise to cooperate with Iranian authorities has not assuaged Iranian concerns. The Iranian reaction has underlined that Pakistan's policy of opportunistic alliances with both sides of the sectarian divide is subject to the law of diminishing returns.

Pakistan desperately needs an economic bailout. Discussions with IMF have been moving slowly. PM Imran Khan's visit to China did not produce significant gains. Imran Khan's second visit to the Kingdom to attend Saudi investment summit brought appreciation from Saudi leadership, at a time when many high profile personalities had cancelled their participation. The visit of the Saudi Crown Prince resulted in signing of MOUs promising $ 20 billion worth of investment in Pakistan.

Pakistan sought to seek closer relations with its western neighbours immediately after independence. The quest for a new identity was a denial of its geography and history rooted in the Indian sub-continent. It also reflected a geo-political calculation to exploit religious ties, pro-Western orientation and proximity to oil-rich States to carve out a special role in the Islamic world. Pakistan was encouraged in this by the British. Basing foreign policy on ties with the Ummah was a natural extension of a policy of seeking nationhood based on religion. Pakistan was very successful in reaping rich economic dividends from its Arab and Iranian benefactors.

Iran became the first country to diplomatically recognise Pakistan as an independent country and the Shah of Iran was the first foreign Head of State to visit Pakistan in 1950.[1] Iran and Pakistan signed a border agreement and settled the border by 1958-59. This helped Pakistan buttress its claim to an area where both the ruler and the people had disputed accession to Pakistan. Iran under the Shah emerged as the largest bilateral donor to Pakistan, providing US$ 800 million in loans and credits between 1974 and 1976.[2]

Pakistan did not neglect the Arab regimes. In fact, Jinnah went beyond governments to seek guidance from Islamic scholars. As Dr. Ayesha Siddiqa, a renowned Pakistani scholar has noted, he wrote to the founder of the Muslim Brotherhood, Sheikh Hassan al-Banna. "I am writing to you, the great Muslim leader, to inform you that I am determined, by God's will, to save Pakistan from the tyranny of imperialism and the various hostile currents." Jinnah added that "I have therefore decided to follow the advice you kindly gave me in your recent letter that my government should assume a purely Islamic character and work in close cooperation with the other strong international Islamic organisations which are headed by your Ikhwan-al-Muslimun society [the Muslim Brotherhood]." Over a period of time, the Muslim Brotherhood would come to be seen as a threat by many Arab states, and is currently the source of a divide between Saudi Arabia, the UAE and Egypt on one hand and Qatar and Turkey on the other hand.

As long as both Iran and Saudi Arabia were part of the American block, their competition was restrained making it easier for Pakistan to seek economic rewards from both. With the Iranian revolution and the Soviet invasion of Afghanistan in 1979, there was a qualitative change in the situation. During the Afghan jehad, Saudi Arabia matched dollar for dollar assistance received by Pakistan from the USA. This also coincided with Zia's policy of introducing Shariat law in Pakistan. Increased Islamisation of Pakistan gave rise to a sectarian rift within society.

Imposition of Shariat law by Zia-ul-Haq in the 1980s gave rise to the Tehrik-e-Nifaz-e-Fiqh-e-Jafaria (TNFJ), a Shia organisation. Sunni groups received more money from the Gulf States than Iran. The policy had the tacit backing of the Pakistan Army, whose favourite Hikmatyar was eventually replaced by the even more rabid Taliban. Encouragement to jehad and reliance upon sectarian organisations brought generous funding to the ISI to pursue Pakistan's geo-political goals in Afghanistan. But the blowback effect has scarred Pakistan polity and affected its relations with both Iran and Afghanistan. Saudi-Iran competition extends to Pakistan's domestic politics.

The Pakistan military has continued Zia's philosophy of relying upon religion to subdue sub-nationalism in Balochistan. During past few years, there has been an influx of extremist Sunni organisations in the border province. If the military's target was Baloch nationalism, the by-product has been an attack on Shia minorities in the province. Whether attacks on Iranian civil and military targets across the border are an unintended consequence, or result of encouragement from outside sources, is difficult to say.

Iran's reaction is to build a 780-km three-foot thick wall with Pakistan despite having a settled border. After the recent attack, Major General Qassem Soleimani, the Commander of the Quds Force of Iran's Islamic Revolution Guards Corps (IRGC), said "It worries Iran that the Pakistani nation and government allow Saudi money to end up in the hands of these Takfiri terrorists'.³ In the past, Iran has lodged complaints in the UN Security Council against terror attacks in Iranian territory by groups based on Pakistani soil.

During the Saudi Crown Prince's visit in February 2019, the joint statement signed by Pakistan and Saudi Arabia mentioned 'total investment *opportunities*' (Italics mine) of over USD 20 billion.⁴ The wording suggests that this is not a firm commitment, but initial identification of possibilities. One of such projects is a LNG re-gassifiction plant in Gwader. The net result of relying upon imported LNG, rather than piped gas from Iran, would be accentuating Pakistan's import dependency on an expensive source of energy. The political fall-out is to block the prospects of reviving the Iran-Pakistan gas pipeline deal signed in 2013.

Locating the LNG re-gassification plant away from sources of consumption in Sindh and Punjab, which together account for 80 per cent of Pakistan's population, to Gwader does not make economic sense. It only reflects Pakistan's objective of involving Saudi Arabia in its strategic project with China. CPEC finds a prominent place in the text of the joint statement issued at the end of the Saudi Crown Prince's visit.

While investment opportunities may or may not fructify, Pakistan has made tangible economic gains from Saudi Arabia. This includes $ 3 billion of deposit placed with the State Bank of Pakistan to shore up Pakistani currency. This also includes $ 3 billion in terms of deferred payment facility for import of crude oil. Imran Khan made two quick visits to Saudi Arabia in September and October soon after assuming office. Though Iran had invited Imran Khan to visit Tehran immediately after his election, this visit took place in April 2019—eight months after Imran Khan's inauguration. He undertook a visit to Saudi Arabia within a month of assuming charge of the office of Prime Minister.

Pakistan's imports from Iran were $327.18 million in 2017, as against imports worth $2.73 billion from Saudi Arabia in the same year according to the World Bank. Pakistan's exports to Iran were 26.53 million in 2017 as against exports of $334.509 million to Saudi Arabia in the same year. Two-way trade with Saudi Arabia is nine times higher than trade with Iran. This is not an isolated trend. Five years ago in 2013, trade with Saudi Arabia was 19 times the trade with Iran. In the normal case, it would be logical to expect the figures to be the other way around. Proximity should reduce freight cost, and make Iranian imports cheaper.

Pakistan's Trade with Iran Thousand US Dollars

	Imports	Exports	Trade Balance
2013	167,777.13 (0.38%)	62,635.21 (0.25%)	-105.141.92
2014	185.730.56 (0.39%)	43,048.79 (0.17%)	-148.681.77
2015	260,894.41 (0.59%)	32,292.99 (0.15%)	-228,601.42
2016	323,085.52 (0.69%)	35,561.94 (0.17%)	-287,523.58
2017	327,180.28 (0.57%)	26,534.41 (0.12%)	-300,645.87

Pakistan's Trade with Saudi Arabia

	Imports	Exports	Trade Balance
2013	3,847,222.35 (8.79%)	494,058.81 (1.97)	-3,353,163.54
2014	4,417,353.76 (9.29%)	509,698.18 (2.06)	-3,907,655.59
2015	3,006,751.39 (6.84%)	431,307.06 (1.95%)	-2,575,444.33
2016	1,843,133.47 (3.92%)	380,435.15 (1.85%)	-1,462,698.33
2017	2,730,371.30 (4.75%)	334,509.63 (1.53%)	-2,395,861.68

Source: World Bank

The vast difference in trade volumes reflects the fact that Pakistan stopped buying Iranian crude around 2010. This was just around the time the last round of sanctions was imposed against Iran. While India sustained crude purchase from Iran, though at a reduced level, Pakistan diverted the sourcing of around 48,000 barrels per day crude from Iran to Kuwait. While normal trade moves through private sector channels, crude oil purchase decisions are essentially made at the government level.

Saudi Arabia established the Islamic Military Counter Terrorism Coalition (IMCTC), popularly known as Islamic NATO on 15 December 2015. It was set up in the wake of the break-out of the Yemen war. It is also supposed to be a bulwark against Iranian expansion in the area. Saudi Arabia and the UAE initially gave Pakistan the cold shoulder in view of Pakistan's refusal to provide ground forces to fight in Yemen. Since then, Pakistan has provided a contingent and former Army Chief Raheel Sharif has been appointed to head the force. Iran sees the mechanism aimed against her.

The refusal to contribute troops to Yemen was justified (i) in terms of Pakistan's policy in avoiding entanglement in intra-Arab or intra-Muslim quarrels, and (ii) specifically on Pakistani Parliament's resolution. The first argument ignores a historical precedent. The Pakistani Army contingent led by Zia-ul-Haq was involved in a civil war in Jordan in 1970, which resulted in the massacre of thousands of Palestinians. The actions of the then Brigadier Zia earned him the job of Army chief later. At a critical stage when Bhutto was debating selection of the next Army chief, King Hussain, at Zia's request, made a call to the Pakistani premier clinching the decision in Zia's favour. The second argument does not reflect the realities of Pakistan's politics. Under Pakistan's constitution, the decision to commit troops lie with the government. With or without the civilian government's consent, the ultimate arbiter is the Army. The matter was referred to Parliament by the Nawaz Sharif government to find political cover to refuse the request from close allies—Saudi Arabia and the UAE, who strongly criticized Pakistan's decision. What the two episodes show is that Pakistan's policy is completely opportunistic.

A special relationship with Saudi Arabia and the Gulf monarchies has been prized by successive Pakistani governments. It is especially popular with the Army. The policy dates back to the 1960s. The Army gets comfortable allowances. The country gets Saudi money. This dependency will deepen in future if Pakistan's economic condition continues to worsen. At the moment, there is no sign of improvement.

While Pakistan's calculation in providing a mercenary army to the Middle East governments is understood, the Saudi advantage is less than clear. The Gulf monarchies faced an existential challenge when Saddam Hussain's army over-ran Kuwait. The military protection to the Kingdom was provided by the American forces. Pakistan's Chief of Army Staff, General Mirza Aslam Beg, gave a call for 'strategic defiance' of the West. This public declaration of hostility was odd, coming as it did from an ally, which had received generous Saudi financial support in return for providing troops for the safety of the Kingdom.

If the Pakistan Army chief publically went against his civilian government and Saudi interest during the first Gulf war, would the presence of a Pakistani contingent in the Kingdom and General Raheel Sharif at the head of the Islamic NATO, serve Saudi security interests in future? If Pakistan did not contribute troops for Yemen, it will be even more reluctant to be drawn into a war with Iran, with whom it has a shared border.

Apart from economic benefits and the provision of military contingents in the service of Saudi Arabia, the third dimension of Pakistan-Saudi relations is Afghanistan. This too has a fall-out on Pakistan-Iran relations. While Saudi Arabia was one of the three states to recognise the Taliban government in the 1990s, Iran supported the Northern Alliance. Today, all three—Pakistan, Iran and Saudi Arabia—together with Russia, are supporting the Taliban. But this coalition is based on expediency and may not be sustained after the withdrawal of American troops from the country.

During the Cold War years, Pakistan and Saudi Arabia were US allies, while Iran was on the opposite side of the ideological divide. But they were united in their common opposition to the Soviet presence in Afghanistan. The Soviet withdrawal led to a re-alignment. This time, the equations are even more curious. Saudi Arabia remains aligned with the USA despite occasional strains. Pakistan is practically allied with Russia and China. Iran could not have any long-term interest in seeing an extremist Sunni organisation like the Taliban come to power in Afghanistan. It shares Russian interest to see the USA withdraw. The US withdrawal could test and expose these tactical alliances. It will bring Iran face to face with a resurgent Taliban on its eastern flank. The threat from extremist Sunni groups across the Baloch border would be multiplied and extend northwards on Iran's border with Afghanistan.

Pakistan provided enrichment technology to Iran in the early 1980s.[5] Has this improved the security of Saudi Arabia or the Gulf monarchies? After testing in 1998, Pakistan claims to have reversed its policy of nuclear proliferation and jealously guards its status as the only Muslim country to have nuclear weapons. While Iran continues to suffer from sanctions, Pakistan has got away with generous aid. The argument in her case is that a nuclear state cannot be allowed to fail. The underlying assumption being that failure would result in nuclear assets falling into the hands of jehadis. This curious logic ignores the fact that the rise of the Taliban in the 1990s and sanctuary to Osama bin Laden and Mullah Umar in Pakistan would not have been possible without the Pakistan Army turning a blind eye. The Pak Army is the ultimate custodian of nuclear weapons.

Iran sees Pakistan aligned with Saudi Arabia at a time of rising sectarian tensions between the two countries. Pakistan certainly has moved closer to Saudi Arabia, though it may not contribute to the security interests of the latter as her response to the first Gulf war and the recent Yemen crisis showed.

NOTES

1. Ammar Ali Qureshi, "Neighbours of many surprises", *The Friday Times*, Lahore, December 2, 2016.
2. Ibid.
3. "Iran's Soleimani warns Pakistan against Saudi attempts to destroy it", Press TV, Tehran, February 21, 2019.
4. For details, see https://www.spa.gov.sa.
5. Adrian Levy and Catherine Scott-Clark, *Deception*, 2007, Bloomsbury, London, p. 136.

22

Conclusion: The Road Ahead

Tilak Devasher

Where would Pakistan be a year from now? What would be the status of Indo-Pak relations during this period?

Crystal ball gazing in the case of Pakistan and Indo-Pak relations is always fraught with risks. There are too many moving parts. As the past has shown, a sudden international event can make Pakistan once more an important player on the regional stage leading to its tattered economy being bolstered yet again. An out-of-the-box initiative by an Indian or Pakistani leader could pave the way for a dialogue.

Despite this, at the time of writing, the portents for either Pakistan or Indo-Pak relations are not very bright.

Pakistan's economy is in a dismal condition. According to the Pakistan Economic Survey 2018-19, GDP growth in 2018-19 had slowed to 3.3 per cent against a projected target of 6.2 per cent and against 5.5 per cent in 2017-18; agricultural growth was down to 0.8 per cent compared to a targeted 3.8 per cent and against last year's 3.9 per cent and industrial growth was down to 1.4 per cent against a targeted 7.6 per cent and against last year's 4.9 per cent. This alarming deceleration of the economy is accompanied by a widening fiscal deficit, massive revenue collection shortfalls and the depreciation of the Pakistan rupee from about Rs 120 to the dollar in July 2018 to Rs 160 in July 2019. This has resulted in an increase in the debt servicing cost as well as inflationary pressures.

The front-loaded tough conditions of the IMF would lead to enormous hardships for the people due to substantial increases in the rates of electricity and gas and withdrawal of subsidies. With exports stagnant, high imports, inelastic revenue collection and growing inflation, Pakistan is in a serious economic crisis. Add to this, the potential 'black-listing' by the Financial Action Task Force in case Pakistan does not get its anti-terror financing and anti-money laundering laws and practices in order, the nature of the crisis can well be fathomed.

One visible sign of the economic downturn is that the defence expenditure during the next fiscal year is slated to remain unchanged as compared to the outgoing fiscal year. Though some have interpreted this to mean that the military had "voluntarily agreed" to cut its expenditure, in reality, no cuts are involved. Instead, as the army chief clarified, the armed forces were "forgoing routine increase in annual defence budget." Even though the army is adept in hiding defence expenditure in the civilian budget, it is obvious that the economic downturn will affect the army too in the long run.

Many would, no doubt, say that Pakistan has been in such a situation before and has been bailed out because it is too important to fail. The argument is that the international community cannot afford Pakistan to fail given its nuclear arsenal, strategic location and an increasingly radicalized polity. These are valid arguments and indeed Pakistan has been surviving for decades by leveraging its geographical position and by threatening to self-destruct.

While the jury is out on whether the international community has the stomach for another bailout given the global slump and fatigue witnessed the world over, the fact still remains that governance in Pakistan is at a low ebb. Outsiders cannot come and rectify Pakistan's governance systems. This is something that Pakistan's leadership would have to do by itself. The starting point would be to accept the responsibility of successive governments—civil and military—in running Pakistan to the ground over the decades. Unfortunately, there is no evidence that there is any such acceptance. It is the same rhetoric that Pakistan's crumbling position is due to an international conspiracy to neutralise Pakistan's nuclear weapons and that the world owes Pakistan for the sacrifices it has made.

Against such a backdrop Pakistan, a year later, is probably going to be in similar dire economic straits, if not worse. The IMF bail-out would be like putting Pakistan on a ventilator, keeping it going but without the heft to implement structural changes needed to resuscitate the economy on a long-term basis. While the China Pakistan Economic Corridor is likely to continue, the Chinese will increasingly find Pakistan's inability to re-pay loans and interest to be a major constraint. Despite this, Pakistan's 'all-weather' relationship with China would continue to grow and strengthen.

Politically, having 'selected' Imran Khan as a replacement for Nawaz Sharif who was getting troublesome by questioning its choices, it is unlikely that the army will pull the rug from under his feet so soon. Hence, civil-military relations in the short-term are likely to be smoother than they have been for a long time. However, two caveats would be necessary. The first is that Imran Khan does not start getting ideas that he is the effective chief executive of Pakistan and starts acting like one, especially in areas that the army considers its preserve. He would, in that case, find himself in a very difficult position. Second, the army expects Imran Khan to perform in the economic sphere. The army would not expect miracles but would certainly expect easing of the economic crisis. The first year of Imran Khan's premiership has not given any confidence that either he or his team has the vision or the competence to actually do so. This would be worrisome for the army.

2018-19 saw two different kinds of movements in Pakistan that have implications for the future. The first, that actually came to the fore in 2017 and gathered momentum later, was the Tehreek-i-Labaik signalling the rise of Barelvi assertion. Even though it has become quiescent in the last few months following the detention of its leadership, the Barelvis have sensed power and influence and they are unlikely to renounce it so quickly. More could well be heard about them in the years to come.

The other is a rights movement of the Pashtuns spearheaded by the Pashtun Tahaffuz Movement and led by Pashtun youth. The Pashtuns have been at the receiving end of violence and dislocation for decades in furtherance of the army's foreign policy agenda in Afghanistan. The Pashtun youth seem to have drawn a line and are asking for an end to the decades-long violence, being treated as cannon fodder and demanding rights as Pakistani citizens under the constitution. This movement is extremely uncomfortable for the army that has traditionally been suspicious of ethnic movements, seeing them as challenging the sovereignty of the state. A confrontation is brewing and quite possibly the Pashtun protests would occupy attention in the year to come.

Indo-Pak relations are likely to continue to flounder on the issue of Pak support to terrorism in Kashmir and other parts of India. Unless and until Pakistan gives up such support to terrorist organisations in letter and spirit and dismantles the terror infrastructure there will be very little forward movement in the relationship. There may be the odd initiative from either side but sooner or later it will come up against the wall of Pakistan's support to terrorism. India does not seem to be in a hurry to enter into a dialogue and could well resort to a policy of calibrated and sequential response to the repeated offers of a dialogue from a beleaguered Pakistan.

Index

#PashtunLongMarch, 66

Aasia Bibi, 33-36
Aasiya Noreen case, 32
Abbasi, Shahid Khaqan, 118
Abdullah, Dr. Abdullah, 145
Afghan Army, 137
Afghan Security Forces, 132
Afghan Society, Changes, 133
Afghanistan, 66-68, 131-32, 134, 136, 138-39, 143, 150
    Future Engagement with, 133
    International Contact Group, 134
Afghanistan-Pakistan Action Plan for Peace and Solidarity (APAPPS), 137, 145
Afghanistan-Pakistan Relations
    Border Fencing, 141-42
    Economic, 143-45
    Peace Talks, 142-43
    Pashtun Issue, 139-40
    Refugee Issue, 137-38
Afghanistan-Pakistan Transit Trade Agreement (APTTA), 143
Afzal Qadri, 37
Agarwal, S.P., *Modern History of Jammu Kashmir: Ancient Times to Shimla Agreement*), 121
Ahl-e-Hadith sect of Sunni Islam, 25, 28
Air Blue, 45
Air Chief Marshal Mujahid Anwar Khan, 110
Al Jehad Trust case, 122
Ali Wazir, 67
Ali, Chaudhry Nisar, 44-45
All of Government, 129
Allah, Army and America, 149
Allah-o-Akbar Tehreek (AAT), 8, 23, 86
Al-Qaeda, 74, 132, 135
Amb. G. Parthasarthy, 96
Ameerul Mujahideen, 24
AML/CFT, 72-73
Anti-Soviet jihad, 29
Anti-Terrorism Act (ATA), 23

Anwar, Rao, 49
Arman Luni death, 63
Armed Forces Special Powers Act (AFSPA), 127
Asad Kharal, 7
Asad Umar, 15
Ashiana Housing Scheme, 44
Asian Development Bank (ADB), 15, 82-83
Awami Action Committee, 118
Awami National Party (ANP), 13, 24, 49, 55, 60

Back Channel, 98-102
Bajwa Doctrine, 92
Balakote, 104-05, 110-11, 113-14, 128
Baloch National Party (BNP), 14
Balochistan Awami Party (BAP), 4, 14
Balochistan, 66
Barelvi, 25, 28-30
BBC, 56, 114
Benazir, 38
Beyond-visual-range (BVR) retarder bombs, 128
Bilawal Bhutto, 91
Brig (Retd) Nauman Saeed, 42
Brig Ejaz Shah, 151
Brig Kamran Khurshid, 42

Central Reserve Police Force (CRPF), 105, 128
Chabahar Port, 134
Chao Phrya Dialogue, 96
China, 93, 158
China Pakistan Economic Corridor (CPEC), 76, 85, 117, 119, 151, 155, 160
    Loans, 81
China-Pakistan relationship, 87
Civil-Military Relations, 4, 85, 88
Civil-Military Struggle, 8
Cold War, 158
Comeback kid, 39
Current Account Deficit (CAD), 80, 86

Da Sang Azadi Da?, 59
Damocles Sword, 42

Dawn, 7, 41-42, 68, 76, 86
Death, destruction, and displacement, 55
Deobandi, 25, 28-29, 31
DGISPR, 107, 113
Director-General Inter-Services Public Relations, 107
Domestic debt and liabilities, 77
Durand agreement, 139
Durand Line, 139, 144

Egypt, 154
Election Commission of Pakistan (ECP), 8, 23
European Union (EU), 74
Exit Control List (ECL), 35-36
Extending a hand of friendship, 102
External borrowings, 78
External debt, 77
Extra-terrestrials, 12

Falah-e-Insaniat Foundation (FIF), 109
FATA Interim Governance Regulation 2018, 57
Federally Administered Tribal Areas (FATA), 48-50, 53, 139-40
Feminism Degrades Motherhood, 19
Financial Action Task Force (FATF), 8, 26, 72-73, 85-86, 88, 93, 114
    Black list, 86
Fiscal Profligacy, 78
Foreign Exchange (forex), 77
Forex Borrowings, 79
Free and Fair Election Network (FAFEN), 16
Freedom of Expression (Media) and Judiciary, 3
Frontier Crimes Regulations (FCR), 57, 139
Full spectrum deterrence, 87

G2G framework, 101
G-7, 72
Gen Abdul Raziq Achekzai, 142
Gen Abdul Waheed Kakar, 39
Gen Karamat, 40
Gen Mirza Aslam Beg, 157
Gen Qamar Javed Bajwa, 56, 63, 92
Gen Yahya Khan, 69
Gen Zia-ul-Haq, 35, 38, 45, 129, 154
General Sales Taxes (GST), 81
Geo News, 7
Geo-politics, 15
Ghani, Ashraf, 66, 136, 141
Gilgit-Baltistan (GB), 117-18, 120
    Council, 118, 123
    Empowerment and Self-Governance Order 2009, 120
    Order, 2018, 119, 122
    Supreme Appellate Court, 119
Gokhale, Vijay Keshav, 105

Golden year, 99
Gul Bukhari, 61

Heart of Asia Process, 134
Hingorani, Aman, *Unravelling the Kashmir Knot*, 121
Human Rights Commission of Pakistan, 3
Hybrid War, 57

Indian Air Force (IAF), 105
Indian Army, 126
Indo-Pak relations, 87, 161
Indus Waters Treaty (IWT), 109
Internally Displaced Persons (IDPs), 55
International Monetary Fund (IMF), 14-15, 79-81, 83, 86, 88, 160
International Press Institute, 7
Iran, 152-53, 157-58
Iran's Islamic Revolution Guards Corps (IRGC), 153-54
Iranian Chabahar Port, 144
Iran-Pakistan gas pipeline, 155
Islamic Democratic Alliance (IDA), 39
Islamic Military Counter Terrorism Coalition (IMCTC), 156
Islamic NATO, 156-57

J&K, 126-27, 129
Jaish-e-Mohammad (JeM), 74, 104-6, 128
Jamaat-e-Islami (JI), 31, 34, 25
Jamaat-ud Dawa (JuD), 23, 34, 56
Jamaat-ulema Pakistan (JUP), 34
Jamiat Ulema-e-Islam-Fazl (JUI-F), 12, 25, 31, 34, 49, 139
Jamiat Ulema-e-Pakistan (JUP), 24-25
Jammat-ud-Dawa (JuD), 109
Jang Group, 7
Jinnah, 153

Kartarpur Corridor, 87
Kashmiri Soldiers, 126
Kasuri, Khurshid Mahmud
    Neither Hawk nor Dove: An Insider's Account of Pakistan's Foreign Policy, 100
Khan, Ahmad Raza, 28
Khan, Dera Ismail, 54
Khan, Ilyas, 56
Khan, Imran, 7, 9, 15-16, 22, 34-35, 42, 44, 76, 88, 91, 93-94, 106-09, 112, 138, 155, 161
    Government, 35, 44, 80, 88
    Visited China, 153
Khan, Jihadi, 92
khatm-i-nabuwat, 24
Khattak, Ali Kuli Khan, 40
Khwaja Asif, 45

Index

Khyber Pakhtunkhwa (KPK), 5, 13, 18, 22, 25, 57, 66, 91, 105, 128, 139
King's Party, 38-39

Lady Bushra Maneka@-Pinky Peer, 44
Lashkar-e-Taiyyaba (LeT), 23, 100, 106
Law Enforcement Agencies (LEAs), 74
Line of Control (LoC), 111, 125, 128
LNG re-gassification plant, 155
Lt Gen Khalid Nawaz Malik, 40
Lt. Gen Khwaja Ziauddin Butt, 40

Maj Gen Asif Ghafoor, 41, 64, 112
Maj Gen Muhd Riaz Abbasi, 45
Maj Gen Qassem Soleimani, 154
Manzoor Pashteen, 54, 56
Markazi Jamiat Ahle Hadith (MJAH), 25, 34
Maryam Nawaz, 42, 45
Media, 3, 7, 9, 41, 56
Media Cell, 41
Mehsud Pashtun, 54
Mehsud, Dr Said Alam, 51
Mehsud, Naqeebullah, 49, 62
Military, 87-88
Military's Dictatorial Role, 8
Milli Muslim League (MML), 8, 23, 25
Modi, Narendra, Prime Minister of India, 94, 105, 109, 129
Mohajir Qaumi Movement, 57
Mohsin Dawar, 67
Montville, 96
Montville, Joseph V., 95
Moscow Format Consultations, 134
Movement for Restoration of Democracy, 38
Muavia Azam, 19
Musharraf-Vajpayee joint statement, 102
Muttahida Majlis-e-Amal (MMA), 4, 13, 22, 25, 141
Muttahida Qaumi Movement-Pakistan (MQM-P), 4-5, 13, 24

Naqvi, Allama Sajid, 25
Nasir, Jibran, 50
National Accountability Bureau, 42
National Conference, 127
National Democratic Alliance Government, 93
National Security Committee (NSC), 106
Nawaz, Asif, 39
Naya Pakistan, 6, 9, 17, 43, 85, 108, 115
Neemrana, 97
Nescoll Limited, 42
New York Times, 54, 56
Nielsen Enterprises Limited, 42

Operation All Out, 126-27

Operation Zarb-e-Azab, 55

Pakhtunkhwa Milli Awami Party (PkMAP), 49
Pakistan, 37-38, 51, 66, 68, 85-86, 93, 106, 108-09, 114, 125, 136, 138, 142-43, 153, 155, 157-58, 160
  Afghan Refugees in, 137-38
  Army, 20, 35, 63-64, 66, 91, 94, 111, 141, 158
  Blasphemy law, 36
  Budget Deficit, 77
  Foreign Office, 110
  GDP, 77, 78
  Military Academy, 150
  Military and Intelligence, 29
  Navy, 87
Pakistan Air Force (PAF), 87, 105, 110, 112-13
Pakistan Bureau of Statistics (PBS), 81
Pakistan Muslim League Quad-e-Azam (PML-Q), 4, 6
Pakistan Muslim League, 40
Pakistan Muslim League-Nawaz (PML-N), 3, 6, 12-13, 18, 77, 91
Pakistan People's Party (PPP), 4, 6, 12, 19, 32, 40, 45, 57, 91
Pakistan Tehreek-e-Insaf (PTI), 3-5, 12-13, 18, 23, 35, 42-44, 49, 76-78, 91-92
Pakistan's
  Economy, 14, 159
  Exports to Iran, 155
  External debt, 15
  First past the post (FPTP) voting system, 27
  Fiscal deficit, 14
  Foreigner's Act, 138
  Imports from Iran, 155
  Relations with China, 88
  Trade with Iran, 156
  Trade with Saudi Arabia, 156
Pakistani Citizenship Act of 1951, 138
Pakistani Pashtun, 59
Pakistan-Occupied Jammu and Kashmir (POJK), 106
Pan Islamism, 130
Panama Papers case, 42
Pashtun, 66
  Diaspora, 53
  Long March, 49
Pashtun Tahafuz Movement (PTM), 53, 140
  Demands, 59
  Impact, 61
  Nature, 60
Pashtun Tahafuz Movement (PTM), 53-58, 63-68, 140
  Agitation, 62
Pashtunkhwa Milli Awami Party (PkMAP), 60, 139

Peoples Democratic Party (PDP), 127
Periodic Corps Commanders, 106
Pervez Elahi, 44
Pirs, 30
Prisoner of War (POW), 106
Proof of Registration (PoR) cards, 138
Pugwash Conference, 96-97
Pulwama terrorist attack, 107, 115, 128

Qatar, 154
Quadrilateral Coordination Group, 134
Qureshi, Shah Mahmood, 108-09, 111, 114

Religious and Extremist Factions, 86
Religious and Extremist Parties, 9
Rising Kashmir, 127
Rizvi, Khadim Hussain, 34
Russia, 158

Safdar Awan, 42
sajda nashins, 30
Sajjad Ali Shah, 40
Salam, Qazi Muhammad, 36
Saleem Safi, 69
Salman Taseer, 29, 34
Saudi Arabia, 152, 154, 157-58
SCO-Afghanistan Contact Group, 134
Security Forces (SF), 125-26
Senator Barrister Mohammad Ali Saif, 57
Sethi, Najam, 21
Shah, Nasim Hassan, 39
Shahbaz, Hamza, 45
Shaikh, Abdul Hafiz, 83
Sharif, Hasan Nawaz, 42
Sharif, Nawaz, 14, 31-32, 38, 42, 43, 91
Sharif, Shahbaz, 16
Sheikh Hassan al-Banna, 153
Siachen, 101
Siddiqa, Dr. Ayesha, 153
SIGAR Report, 144
Singh, S.K., 96
Sir Creek, 101
Siraj-ul-Haq, 25
Special Drawing Rights (SDR) Quota, 81
Special Police Officers (SPOs), 126
State Bank of Pakistan (SBP), 80

Tahir ul Qadri, 28

Taliban, 15, 49, 54, 60, 61, 64-66, 129, 131-37, 142-43, 145, 150-51
Taliban Khan, 92
Tehreek-e-Jafaria, 25
Tehreek-e-Labbaik Pakistan (TLP), 8, 14, 22-24, 26, 29-31, 34, 87
Tehreek-e-Labbaik Ya Rasool Allah (TLYRA), 8, 23, 34
Tehreek-i-Taliban Pakistan (TTP), 19, 65
Tehrik-e-Nifaz-e-Fiqh-e-Jafaria (TNFJ), 154
Terror and Talks, 102
Terror Financing (TF), 73-74, 86
The Guardian, 36
The Nation, 51
The News, 8
Think-tank, 101
Track-1.5, 100-02
Track-II, 101-02
    Diplomacy, 95-96, 99
    Engagements, 98
    Initiatives, 98
    Interactions, 98
Track-One negotiations, 99
Treaty of Gandamak, 139
Trump, Donald, 151
Truth and Reconciliation Commission, 58
Turkey, 154

UK, 101
UN, 8
UNHCR, 138
United Arab Emirates (UAE), 79, 154, 157
United Nations Security Council, 109, 143
US Withdrawal from Afghanistan, 131, 137
USA, 8, 74, 87-88, 101, 132, 134, 142, 158
USA-Japan, 101
USA-West Europe, 101

Vajpayee-Musharraf dialogue, 98
Value Transfer Services (MVTS), 73
Vehicle-Borne Improvised Explosive Device, 105

Wahabi, 28-29, 31
Wajabul Katl, 37
War on Terror, 150
Waziristan, 53, 60, 62-63
West, 131, 157
World Bank, 15, 83, 155